Home Decoration in Crochet

25 COLORFUL DESIGNS
TO BRIGHTEN YOUR HOME

TANYA EBERHARDT

Tuva Publishing

www.tuvapublishing.com

Address: Merkez Mah. Cavusbasi Cad. No:71
Cekmekoy - Istanbul 34782 / Turkey
Tel: +9 0216 642 62 62

Home Decoration in Crochet

First Print: 2017 / September

All Global Copyrights Belongs To
Tuva Tekstil ve Yayıncılık Ltd

Content Crochet

Editor in Chief Ayhan DEMİRPEHLİVAN
Project Editor Kader DEMİRPEHLİVAN
Designer Tanya EBERHARDT
Technical Editor Leyla ARAS, Büşra ESER
Text Editor Wendi CUSINS
Graphic Designers Ömer ALP, Abdullah BAYRAKÇI,
Zilal ÖNEL
Photography Tanya EBERHARDT, Tuva Publishing

ISBN: 978-605-9192-19-4

Printing House
Bilnet Matbaacılık ve Yayıncılık A.Ş.

 TuvaYayincilik  TuvaPublishing
TuvaYayincilik  TuvaPublishing

Contents

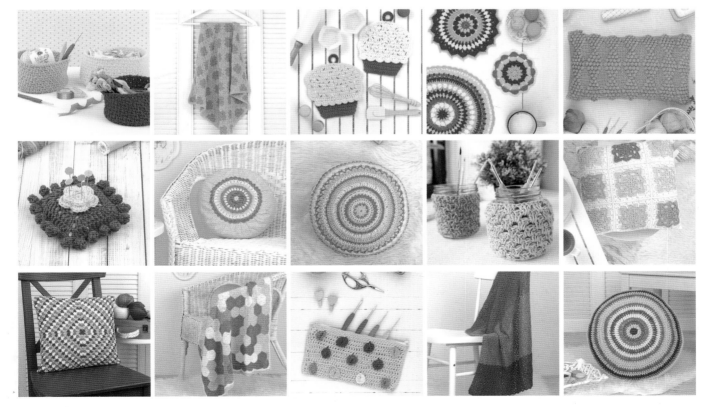

Introduction

As humans, we tend to surround ourselves with things that are precious to us. For me, this is crochet, as if gives me an opportunity to express myself. Crochet is so versatile, you can create almost anything. All you need to get going on a project is one hook and a ball of yarn. And with a bit of practice, you can get hooked!

When designing, I enjoy using decorative and textured stitches while still maintaining the practical function of the finished item. To spark my creativity, I play with colors and shapes as well. By incorporating modern shades in classic crochet, the texture of the different stitches are highlighted.

In this book, I'm sharing lots of home décor ideas – from quick-to-make accessories, to precious gifts for friends and family. Everything you need to create a personal touch that will make any house a home.

Each project is unique and I'm sure you will find the perfect one to keep your hands busy – even if this is your first time picking up a crochet hook. So, gather up your yarn, raise your hook, and get ready for some handmade fun-time!

Projects

Nesting Baskets

These three differently sized baskets nestle perfectly inside each other. They are ideal for storing a variety of household or personal items. Make each one in a bright color or even combine colors together for some extra fun!

Finished Size

Small Basket
3 ½" (9 cm) in diameter
3 ½" (9 cm) height

Medium Basket
4" (10 cm) in diameter
4" (10 cm) height

Large Basket
4 ¾" (12 cm) in diameter
4 ¾" (12 cm) height

Materials

Small Basket
DMC Natura Just Cotton
Main Color – Prussian (#64) - 3 balls

Medium Basket
DMC Natura Just Cotton Yummy
Main Color – Bougainvillea (#93) - 3 balls

Large Basket
DMC Natura Just Cotton Yummy
Main Color – Jaune Indien (#89) - 4 balls

Hook Size H-8 (5.00 mm)

Yarn Needle

Corner to Corner Baby Blanket

This bright and modern lightweight baby blanket is a fun project to make as a special gift for a precious new arrival. Sweet dreams, little one!

Finished Size

About 24 ½" (62 cm) square, after blocking.

Materials

DMC Natura Just Cotton Yummy
Color A – Peach (#104) - 4 balls
Color B – Teal (#99) - 2 balls

Hook: Size D-3 (3.25 mm)

Yarn Needle

PATTERN NOTES

The Corner to Corner (C2C) crochet technique is worked up using 'blocks'. Each block consists of 3 chain stitches and 3 double crochets. The pattern typically starts in the bottom right hand corner, and is worked on the diagonal, increasing each row until desired size, and then decreasing each row, to finish at the opposite (top left hand) corner. A pixel graph is followed row by row diagonally.

Note: The starting yarn tail is the first corner point. Changing colors in C2C is a bit different. When you're changing colors at the start of a new row, you still change the color in the last stitch worked.

When you need to change colors in the middle of the row, you pull the new color through the slip stitch when joining to the ch-3 space. Work over any strands, so that the back of the blanket looks as neat as the front. Leave the yarn hanging and pick it up on the return row. Remember to use different balls/bobbins of yarn, so that no 'stranding' occurs.

SPECIAL STITCHES

Reverse Single Crochet (or Crab Stitch) (rev-sc) – With a loop on the hook, * insert hook in next st to the right and pull up loop, yarn over and pull through both loops on hook. Repeat from * across (or around).

Join With Single Crochet (join with sc) - With slip knot on hook, insert hook into stitch or space indicated and pull up a loop (two loops on hook). Yarn over and pull through both loops on hook (first single crochet made).

BLANKET

ROW 1: (Right Side) Starting with Color A, ch 6, dc in 4th ch from hook, dc in each of next 2 ch (first block made). (1 block)

Increase Rows

ROW 2: Ch 6, turn, dc in 4th ch from hook, dc in each of next 2 ch (second block made), skip next 3 dc, sl st in next ch-3 sp, ch 3, 3 dc in same ch-3 sp (third block made). (2 blocks)

ROW 3: Ch 6, turn, dc in 4th ch from hook, dc in each of next 2 ch, *skip next 3 dc, sl st in next ch-3 sp, ch 3, 3 dc in same ch-3 sp (of 3rd block made in Row 2); rep from * into 2nd block made in Row 2, changing to Color B in last dc (see Changing Colors in Crochet Techniques). (3 blocks)

ROW 4: With Color B, ch 6, turn, dc in 4th ch from hook, dc in each of next 2 ch, *skip next 3 dc, sl st in next ch-3 sp, ch 3, 3 dc in same ch-3 sp*, changing to Color A in next sl st (see Pattern Notes), rep from * to * across, changing to Color B in last dc. (4 blocks)

ROWS 5-40: Continue as established, following the color chart. At the end of Row 40, there will be 40 blocks across.

Decrease Rows

ROW 41: Ch 1, turn, sl st in each of next 2 dc, *sl st in next ch-3 sp, ch 3, 3 dc in same ch-3 sp, skip next 3 dc; rep from * across, following the Color Chart, ending with sl st in last ch-3 sp. (39 blocks)

ROWS 42-78: Following the Color Chart, rep Row 41. At the end of Row 78, there are 2 blocks.

ROW 79: Ch 1, turn, sl st in each of next 2 dc, sl st in next ch-3 sp, ch 3, 3 dc in same ch-3 sp, skip next 3 dc, sl st in last ch-3 sp. (1 block)

Fasten off and weave in all ends.

BORDER

ROW 1: With right side facing, using Color A, join with sc (see Special Stitches) to any corner, 2 sc in same st, evenly sc around blanket, working 3 sc in each corner; join with sl st to first sc.

ROW 2: Ch 1, sc in each sc around; join with sl st to first sc.

ROW 3: Ch 1, rev-sc (see Special Stitches) in each sc around; join with sl st to first st.

Fasten off and weave in all ends.

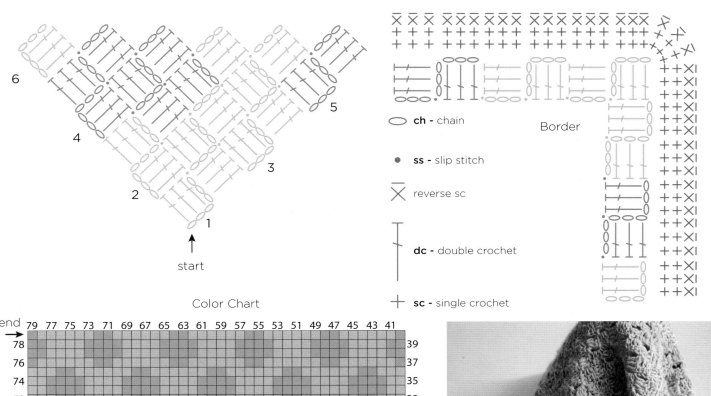

6

4

2

1

↑
start

5

3

Color Chart

ch - chain

ss - slip stitch

⊠ reverse sc

| dc - double crochet

+ sc - single crochet

Border

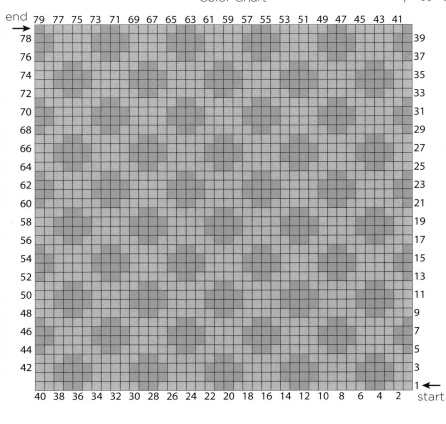

end

| | 79 | 77 | 75 | 73 | 71 | 69 | 67 | 65 | 63 | 61 | 59 | 57 | 55 | 53 | 51 | 49 | 47 | 45 | 43 | 41 | |

78 — 39
76 — 37
74 — 35
72 — 33
70 — 31
68 — 29
66 — 27
64 — 25
62 — 23
60 — 21
58 — 19
56 — 17
54 — 15
52 — 13
50 — 11
48 — 9
46 — 7
44 — 5
42 — 3
— 1 ← start

40 38 36 34 32 30 28 26 24 22 20 18 16 14 12 10 8 6 4 2 start

Cupcake Potholders

These calorie-free special cupcakes are your new kitchen helpers.
Put them to work as potholders, trivets or even placemats.
They're just so versatile and a whole lot of fun. This set would
also make a great gift!

Finished Size

7½" (19 cm) across widest point

8½" (22 cm) long - including hanger

Materials

DMC Natura Just Cotton Medium
Color A – Taupe (#11)
Color B – Pink (#44) or Off-White (#03)
Color C – Red (#55)

Various Colors (small amounts) – for Sprinkles.

Hook Size G-6 (4.00 mm)

Yarn Needle

Stitch Markers

Three Doily Set

Brighten up any home with this trio of colorful doilies in cool cotton. They're perfect as decorative doilies, or use them on your table as placemats and coasters.

Finished Sizes

Small Doily
About 5" (12.5 cm) in diameter

Medium Doily
About 8½" (21.5 cm) in diameter

Large Doily
About 12" (30.5 cm) in diameter

Materials

DMC Natura Just Cotton
Color A – Aqua (#100)
Color B – Gerbera (#98)
Color C – Crimson (#61)
Color D – Prussian (#64)
Color E – Jaune Indien (#89)
Color F – Ivory (#02)
Color G – Glicine (#30)

Hook Size D-3 (3.25 mm)

Yarn Needle

PATTERN NOTES

1. Each color is joined with the right side of the Doily facing, unless otherwise specified.

2. Fasten off at the end of each Round and weave in all ends, unless otherwise instructed.

SPECIAL STITCHES

Beginning Three Double Crochet Bobble (beg-3dcbob): Ch 2, *yarn over, insert hook in same stitch or space and draw up a loop, yarn over, pull through 2 loops on hook; repeat from * once more (3 loops remain on hook), yarn over, pull through all 3 loops on hook (first Bobble made).

Three Double Crochet Bobble (3dcbob): Yarn over, insert hook in stitch or space indicated and draw up a loop (3 loops on hook), yarn over, pull through 2 loops on hook (2 loops on remain on hook), *yarn over, insert hook in same stitch or space and draw up a loop, yarn over, pull through 2 loops on hook; repeat from * once more (4 loops remain on hook), yarn over, pull through all 4 loops on hook.

Join With Single Crochet (join with sc) - With slip knot on hook, insert hook into stitch or space indicated and pull up a loop (2 loops on hook). Yarn over and pull through both loops on hook (first single crochet made).

V-Stitch (v-st): Work (dc, ch 2, dc) in same stitch or space indicated.

Picot: Ch 3, slip stitch into back bar of first chain.

Beginning Double Crochet Bobble (beg-5dcbob): Ch 2, *yarn over, insert hook in same stitch or space and draw up a loop, yarn over, pull through 2 loops on hook; repeat from * 3 times more (5 loops remain on hook), yarn over, pull through all 5 loops on hook (first Bobble made).

Double Crochet Bobble (5dcbob): Yarn over, insert hook in stitch or space indicated and draw up a loop, yarn over, pull through 2 loops on hook, *yarn over, insert hook in same stitch or space and draw up a loop, yarn over, pull through 2 loops on hook; repeat from * 3 times more (6 loops remain on hook), yarn over, pull through all 6 loops on hook.

SMALL DOILY

Color Sequence:

1	Color	A
2	Color	B
3	Color	C
4	Color	D
5	Color	E
6	Color	F
7	Color	G
8	Color	F

ROUND 1: (Right Side) Following the Color Sequence, using first color, ch 4; join with sl st into first ch to form a ring; ch 4 (counts as first dc & ch-1), [dc in ring, ch 1] 11 times; join with sl st to first dc (3rd ch of beg ch-4). (12 dc & 12 ch-1 sps)

ROUND 2: Join next color with sl st to any ch-1 sp, beg-3dcbob (see Special Stitches), ch 2, [3dcbob (see Special Stitches) in next ch-1 sp, ch 2] around; join with sl st to top of first bobble. (12 bobbles & 12 ch-2 sps)

ROUND 3: Join next color with sl st to any ch-2 sp, ch 3 (counts as first dc), 3 dc in same sp, [4 dc in next ch-2 sp] around; join with sl st to first dc (3rd ch of beg ch-3). (48 dc)

ROUND 4: Using next color, join with sc (see Special Stitches) to any sp between 4-dc groups, ch 4, skip next 4 dc, [sc in sp between dc-groups, ch 4, skip next 4 dc] around; join with sl st to first sc. (12 sc & 12 ch-4 lps)

ROUND 5: Join next color with sl st to any ch-4 lp, ch 3 (counts as first dc), 5 dc in same lp, [6 dc in next ch-4 lp] around; join with sl st to first dc (3rd ch of beg ch-3). (72 dc)

ROUND 6: Using next color, join with sc to any sp between 6-dc groups, ch 7, skip next 6 dc, [sc in sp between dc-groups, ch 7, skip next 6 dc] around; join with sl st to first sc. (12 sc & 12 ch-7 lps)

ROUND 7: Using next color, join with sc to any ch-7 lp, (hdc, 5 dc, hdc, sc) in same lp, [(sc, hdc, 5 dc, hdc, sc) in next ch-7 lp] around; join with sl st to first sc. (12 scallops)

ROUND 8: Using next color, join with sc to any st, [sc in next st] around; join with sl st to first sc. (108 sc)
Fasten off and weave in all ends.

MEDIUM DOILY

Color Sequence:

1	Color G	6	Color A	
2	Color E	7	Color C	
3	Color D	8	Color F	
4	Color F	9 & 10	Color D (2 rounds in same color)	
5	Color B	11 Color A		

ROUNDS 1-5: Following the Color Sequence, rep Rounds 1 to 5 of Small Doily.

ROUND 6: Join next color with sl st to any dc, ch 2, hdc in same st as joining, ch 1, skip next dc, [hdc in next dc, ch 1, skip next dc] around; join with sl st to first hdc. (36 hdc & 36 ch-1 sps)

ROUND 7: Join next color with sl st to any ch-1 sp, ch 3 (counts as first dc, now and throughout), dc in same sp, [2 dc in next ch-1 sp] around; join with sl st to first dc (3rd ch of beg ch-3). (72 dc)

ROUND 8: Join next color with sl st to any sp between 2-dc groups, ch 3, 2 dc in same sp, skip next 2 dc, [3 dc in next sp between dc-groups, skip next 2 dc] around; join with sl st to first dc (3rd ch of beg ch-3). (108 dc)

ROUND 9: Join next color with sl st to any sp between 3-dc groups, ch 5 (counts as first dc & ch-2), dc in same sp (first v-st made), skip next 3 dc, [v-st (see Special Stitches) in next sp between dc-groups, skip next 3 dc] around; join with sl st to first dc (3rd ch of beg ch-5). (36 v-sts) DO NOT FASTEN OFF.

ROUND 10: Sl st in next ch-2 sp, ch 3, 6 dc in same sp, sc in next ch-2 sp, [7 dc in next ch-2 sp, sc in next ch-2 sp] around; join with sl st to first dc (3rd ch of beg ch-3). (18 dc-shells & 18 sc)

ROUND 11: Using next color, join with sc to any sc, [sc in each of next 4 dc, picot (see Special Stitches), sc in each of next 3 dc, sc in next sc] around, omitting last sc on final repeat; join with sl st to first sc. (144 sc & 18 picots) Fasten off and weave in all ends.

LARGE DOILY

Color Sequence:

1	Color	D	10	Color	F
2	Color	A	11	Color	A
3	Color	F	12	Color	C
4	Color	B	13	Color	G
5	Color	G	14	Color	D
6	Color	C	15	Color	E
7	Color	E	16	Color	F
8	Color	D	17	Color	B
9	Color	B			

ROUND 1: (Right Side) Following the Color Sequence, using first color, ch 4; join with sl st into first ch to form a ring; ch 4 (counts as first dc & ch-1), [dc in ring, ch 1] 11 times; join with sl st to first dc (3rd ch of beg ch-4). (12 dc & 12 ch-1 sps)

ROUND 2: Join next color with sl st to any ch-1 sp, ch 3 (counts as first dc, now and throughout), dc in same sp, ch 2, [2 dc in next ch-1 sp, ch 2] around; join with sl st to top of first dc. (24 dc & 12 ch-2 sps)

ROUNDS 3-5: Following Color Sequence rep Rounds 3-5 of Small Doily.

ROUNDS 6-9: Following the Color Sequence, rep Rounds 6-9 of Medium Doily.

ROUND 10: Join next color with sl st to any ch-2 sp, beg-5dcbob (see Special Stitches) in same sp, ch 2, [5dcbob (see Special Stitches) in next ch-2 sp, ch 2] around; join with sl st to top of first bobble. (36 bobbles & 36 ch-2 sps)

ROUND 11: Join next color with sl st to any ch-2 sp, ch 3, 2 dc in same sp, [3 dc in next ch-2 sp] around; join with sl st to first dc (3rd ch of beg ch-3). (108 dc)

ROUND 12: Join next color with sl st to any dc, ch 3, [dc in next dc] around; join with sl st to first dc (3rd ch of beg ch-3). (108 dc)

ROUND 13: Join next color with sl st to any dc, ch 3, dc in same dc, skip next dc, [2 dc in next dc, skip next dc] around; join with sl st to first dc (3rd ch of beg ch-3). (108 dc)

ROUND 14: Using next color, join with sc to any sp between 2-dc groups, ch 3, skip next 2 dc, [sc in sp between dc-groups, ch 3, skip next 2 dc] around; join with sl st to first sc. (54 sc & 54 ch-3 lps)

Drawstring Pouch

This handy, hold-all pouch has a striking geometric design, using a simple mesh stitch. The uses for a drawstring bag are endless! When lined with fabric, it makes an ideal project bag - for carrying your yarn and crochet hook. You could also use it as a gift bag, filled with lots of goodies and given to a special friend.

Finished Size

Base – About 8" (20 cm) diameter

Height – About 11" (28 cm)

Materials

DMC Natura Just Cotton
Color A - Brique (#86) 2 balls
Color B - Geranium (#52) 4 balls

Hook Size D-3 (3.25 mm)

Yarn Needle

Fabric for Pouch Lining (optional)

Needle & thread (optional)

Pouch Sides

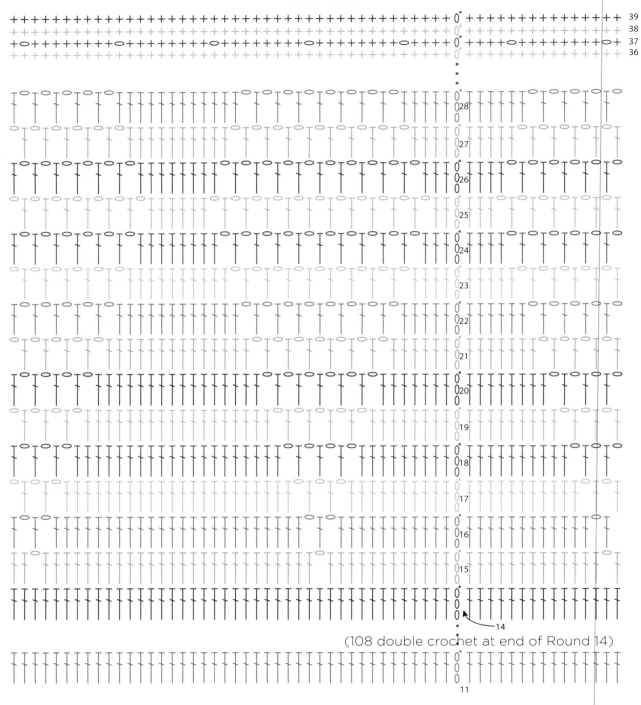

(108 double crochet at end of Round 14)

Pouch Base   (108 double crochet
at end of Round 9)

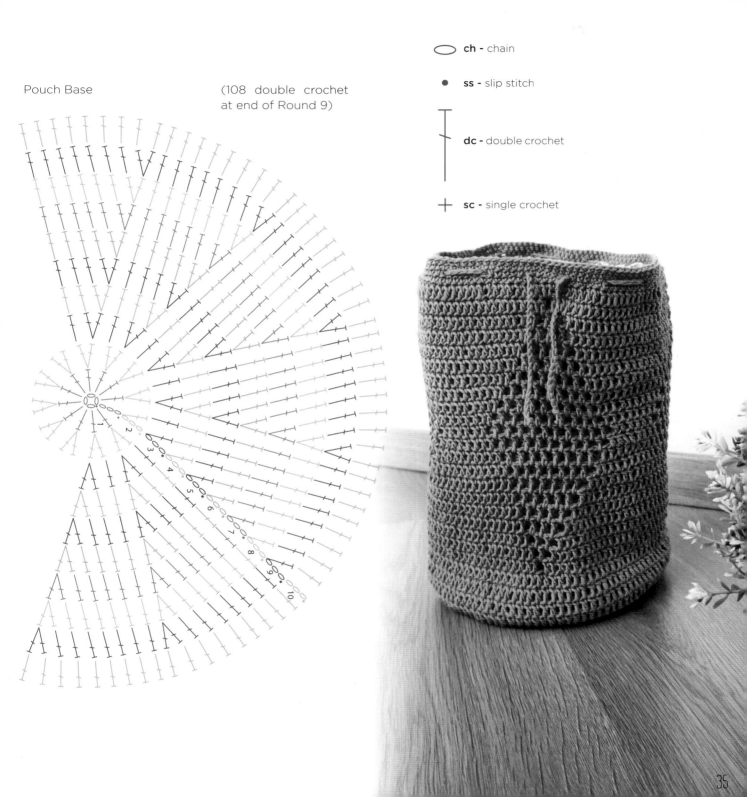

ch - chain

ss - slip stitch

dc - double crochet

sc - single crochet

Flower Pincushion

This darling, floral pincushion will quickly become your favorite go-to partner when sewing. You will never be picking up stray pins again! Use your favorite colors to make one for yourself, and then make many more as gifts for all your crafty friends.

Finished Size

About 3 ½" (9 cm)

Materials

DMC Natura Just Cotton
Color A – Golden Lemon (#43)
Color B – Crimson (#61)

Hook Size D-3 (3.25 mm)

Yarn Needle

Fabric Lining for Cushion

Pincushion insert (or Fiberfill)

Large Flower Appliqued Cushion

A fun and colorful round appliqué, with a flower center, is just what is needed to add a touch of Spring to your home. The bright floral tones used against the green fabric of a cushion cover, will brighten up anyone's mood.

Finished Size

Appliqué measures about 7" (18 cm) in diameter.

Materials

DMC Natura Just Cotton
Color A – Golden Lemon (#43)
Color B – Coral (#18)
Color C – Glicine (#30)
Color D – Ivory (#02)
Color E – Pistache (#13)
Color F – Gerbera (#98)

Hook Size D-3 (3.25 mm)

Yarn Needle

Round Cushion Insert

Fabric for Pillow

Needle & Thread

SPECIAL STITCHES

Join With Single Crochet (join with sc) - With slip knot on hook, insert hook into stitch or space indicated and pull up a loop (2 loops on hook). Yarn over and pull through both loops on hook (first single crochet made).

APPLIQUÉ

ROUND 1: (Right Side) With Color A, ch 4; join with sl st to first ch to form a ring; ch 3 (counts as first dc, now and throughout), 11 dc in ring; join with sl st to first dc (3rd ch of beg ch-3). (12 dc) Fasten off Color A and weave in all ends.

ROUND 2: With right side facing, using Color B, join with sl st to sp between any 2 dc-sts on Rnd 1, ch 1, sc in same sp, 3 dc in next dc, sc in next sp between dc-sts, [sc in next sp between dc-sts, 3 dc in next dc, sc in next sp between dc-sts] around; join with sl st to first sc. (12 sc & 6 petals)

ROUND 3: Working behind petals, [ch 3, skip next petal, sl st in sp between sc-sts] around. (6 ch-3 sps)

ROUND 4: Ch 1, [(sc, 5 dc, sc) in next ch-3 sp] around; join with sl st to first sc. (6 petals)

ROUND 5: Working behind petals, [ch 6, skip next petal, sl-st around post of next sl st] around. (6 ch-6 lps) Fasten off Color B and weave in all ends.

ROUND 6: With right side facing, join Color C with sl st to any ch-6 lp, ch 3, 7 dc in same lp, [8 dc in next ch-6 lp] around; join with sl st to first dc (3rd ch of beg ch-3). (6 petals) Fasten off Color C and weave in all ends.

ROUND 7: With right side facing, join Color D with sl st to any dc on Rnd 6, ch 2, 2 hdc in same st as joining, [ch 1, skip next dc, 2 hdc in next dc] around, ending ch 1, skip last dc; join with sl st to first hdc. (48 hdc & 24 ch-1 sps) Fasten off Color D and weave in all ends.

ROUND 8: With right side facing, join Color E with sl st to any ch-1 sp, ch 3, 2 dc in same sp, skip next 2 hdc, [3 dc in next ch-1 sp, skip next 2 hdc] around; join with sl st to first dc (3rd ch of beg ch-3). (24 groups of 3-dc each) Fasten off Color E and weave in all ends.

ROUND 9: With right side facing, join Color A with sl st to any dc, ch 3, [dc in next dc] around; join with sl st to first dc (3rd ch of beg ch-3). (72 dc) Fasten off Color A and weave in all ends.

ROUND 10: With right side facing, join Color D to any dc, ch 3, dc in same st as joining, skip next dc, [2 dc in next dc, skip next dc] around; join with sl st to first dc (3rd ch of beg ch-3). (36 groups of 2-dc each) Fasten off Color D and weave in all ends.

ROUND 11: With right side facing, using Color F, join with sl st to sp between 2-dc groups, ch 1, sc in same sp, ch 3, [skip next 2 dc, sc in sp between dc-groups, ch 3] around; join with sl st to first sc. (36 sc & 36 ch-3 lps) Fasten off Color F and weave in all ends.

ROUND 12: With right side facing, using Color C, join with sc (see Special Stitches) to any ch-3 lp, (hdc, dc, tr, dc, hdc, sc) in same lp, [(sc, hdc, dc, tr, dc, hdc, sc) in next ch-3 lp] around; join with sl st to first sc. (36 scallops) Fasten off Color C and weave in all ends.

FINISHING – Use photo as guide

Using fabric, cover Cushion insert.
Position Appliqué on cushion, and sew in place.

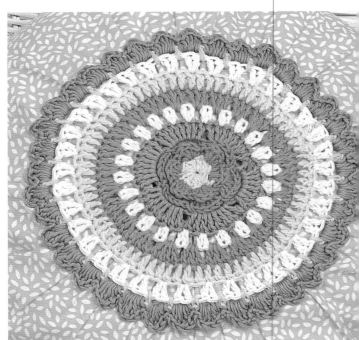

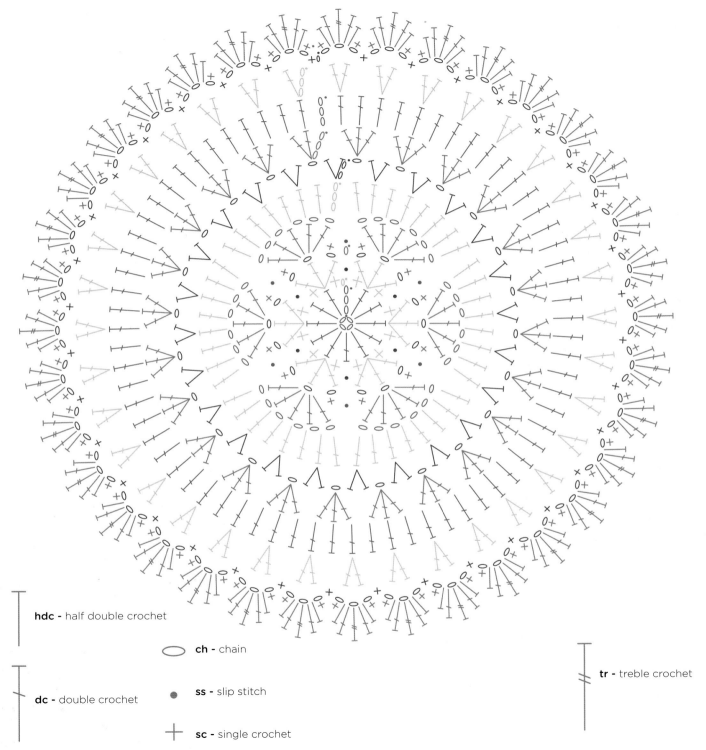

hdc - half double crochet

ch - chain

ss - slip stitch

sc - single crochet

dc - double crochet

tr - treble crochet

43

Fruity Egg Cozies

Celebrate summer fruitiness with these fun, adorable egg cozies. The vibrant colors are sure to brighten up your breakfast table and add a tropical touch.

Finished Size

Each cozy measures about
1 ½" (4 cm) diameter and 2 ½" (6 cm) tall

Materials

DMC Natura Just Cotton
Color A – Ibisa (#01)
Color B – Pistache (#13)
Color C – Siena (#41)
Color D – Passion (#23)
Color E – Crimson (#61)
Color F – Golden Lemon (#43)
For Embroidery – Noir (#11)

Hook Size C-2 (2.75 mm)

Stitch Marker (optional)

Yarn Needle

Black Embroidery Thread and Needle (for Kiwi & Watermelon Cozies)

SPECIAL STITCHES

Beginning Three Double Crochet Bobble (beg-3dcbob):

Ch 2, *yarn over, insert hook in same stitch or space and draw up a loop, yarn over, pull through 2 loops on hook; repeat from * once more (3 loops remain on hook), yarn over, pull through all 3 loops on hook (first Bobble made).

Three Double Crochet Bobble (3dcbob):

Yarn over, insert hook in stitch or space indicated and draw up a loop (3 loops on hook), yarn over, pull through 2 loops on hook (2 loops on remain on hook), *yarn over, insert hook in same stitch or space and draw up a loop, yarn over, pull through 2 loops on hook; repeat from * once more (4 loops remain on hook), yarn over, pull through all 4 loops on hook.

Double Treble (dtr):

Yarn over hook three times, insert hook in stitch or space indicated and draw up a loop (five loops on hook). [Yarn over and pull yarn through two loops on hook] 4 times, until only one loop remains on hook.

BASIC COZY PATTERN (for Kiwi, Apple & Watermelon)

ROUND 1: (Right Side) Starting with first Color, ch 3; join with sl st into first ch to form a ring; ch 1, 6 sc in ring; DO NOT JOIN, mark last st on each round. (6 sc)

ROUND 2: 2 sc in each sc around. (12 sc)

ROUND 3: [2 sc in next sc, sc in next sc] around. (18 sc)

ROUND 4: [2 sc in next sc, sc in each of next 2 sc] around. (24 sc)

ROUND 5: [2 sc in next sc, sc in each of next 3 sc] around. (30 sc)

ROUNDS 6-13: Sc in each sc around. (30 sc) At the end of Round 13, sl st in next sc. Fasten off and weave in all ends.

KIWI EGG COZY

Repeat Basic Cozy Pattern, working as follows.

Color A - Rounds 1 - 3. At the end of Round 3, change color to B in last sc.

Color B - Rounds 4 - 12. At the end of Round 12, change color to C in last sc.

Color C - Round 13.

Finishing – Use photo as guide

With right side of Cozy facing, using the Black thread and needle, embroider 5 back-stitches onto White section of Cozy. Fasten off and weave in all ends.

APPLE EGG COZY

Repeat Basic Cozy Pattern, working as follows.
Color D - Rounds 1 - 13.

Apple Stem

ROUND 1: (Right Side) Using Color C, ch 3; join with sl st into first ch to form a ring; ch 1, 4 sc in ring; DO NOT JOIN, mark last st on each round. (4 sc)

ROUNDS 2-5: Sc in each sc around. (4 sc)
At the end of Round 5, sl st in next sc. Finish off leaving long end for sewing.

Apple Leaf

ROW 1: (Right Side) Using Color B, ch 8, sc in 2nd ch from hook, hdc in next ch, dc in each of next 3 ch, hdc in next ch, (sc, sl st) in last ch. Finish off leaving long end for sewing

Finishing – Use photo as guide

With right side of Cozy facing, using long ends and yarn needle, sew the Stem and Leaf to top of Cozy. Fasten off and weave in all ends.

WATERMELON EGG COZY

Repeat Basic Cozy Pattern, working as follows.

Color E - Rounds 1 - 11. At the end of Round 11, change color to A in last sc.

Color A - Round 12, changing to Color B in last sc.

Color B - Round 13.

Finishing – Use photo as guide

With right side of Cozy facing, using the Black thread and needle, embroider a few back-stitches onto Crimson section of Cozy. Fasten off and weave in all ends.

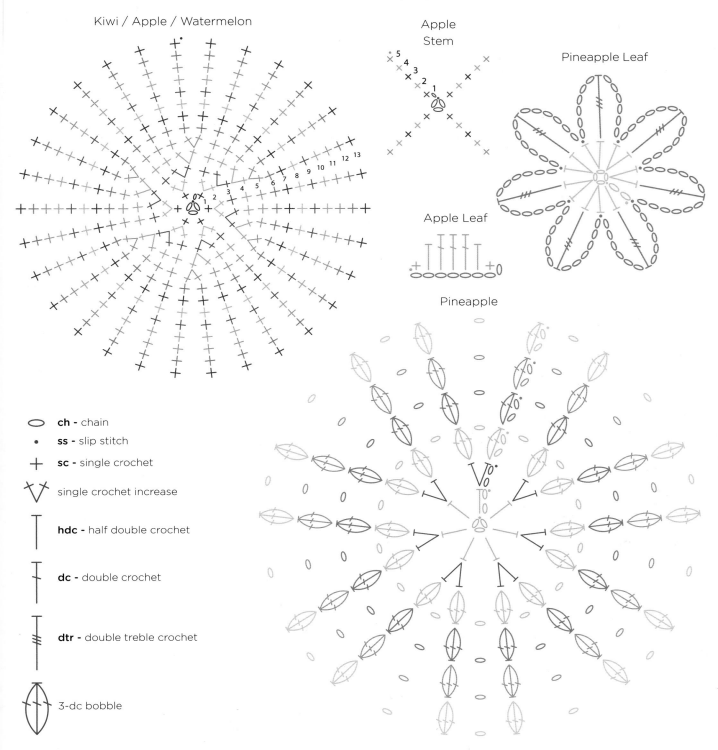

Kiwi / Apple / Watermelon

Apple Stem

Pineapple Leaf

Apple Leaf

Pineapple

⬭ **ch -** chain

• **ss -** slip stitch

✛ **sc -** single crochet

single crochet increase

hdc - half double crochet

dc - double crochet

dtr - double treble crochet

3-dc bobble

PINEAPPLE EGG COZY

ROUND 1: (Right Side) Using Color F, ch 3; join with sl st into first ch to form a ring; ch 2 (does NOT count as first hdc, now and throughout), 7 hdc in ring; join with sl st to first hdc. (7 hdc)

ROUND 2: Ch 2, [2 hdc in next hdc] around; join with sl st to first hdc. (14 hdc)

ROUND 3: Beg-3dcbob (see Special Stitches) in same st as joining, ch 1, [3dcbob (see Special Stitches) in next hdc, ch 1] around; join with sl st to top of first 3dcbob. (14 bobs & 14 ch-1 sps)

ROUNDS 4-6: Beg-3dcbob in same st as joining, ch 1, [3dcbob in top on next 3dcbob, ch 1] around; join with sl st to top of first 3d bob. (14 bobs & 14 ch-1 sps) At the end of Round 6, fasten off and weave in all ends.

Pineapple Leaf

ROUND 1: (Right Side) Starting with a long tail (for sewing), using Color B, ch 4, join with sl st in first ch to form ring; ch 2 (counts as first hdc), 13 hdc in ring; join with sl st to first hdc (2nd ch of beg ch-2). (14 hdc)

ROUND 2: [Ch 6, dtr (see Special Stitches) in next hdc, ch 6, sl st in next hdc] around. (7 leaves) Fasten off and weave in all ends.

Finishing – Use Photo As Guide

With right side of Cozy facing, using long end and yarn needle, sew Pineapple Leaf to top of Cozy.

Geometric Popcorn Cushion Cover

Stitch a striking pillow using a clever geometric pattern. An ideal cushion for cuddling up with on chilly evenings. This beautifully soft bobble cushion is a fabulous way to add a dash of modernity to your living room. Make a few in a variety of colors for some pop!

Finished Size

About 10" (25 cm) wide by 19" (48 cm) long

Materials

DMC Natura Just Cotton
Main Color – Aquamarina (#25) 5 balls

Hook Size D-3 (3.25 mm)

Yarn Needle

Rectangular Cushion Insert -
10" (25 cm) wide by 19" (48 cm) long

Fabric for covering Cushion

Needle & Thread

PATTERN NOTES

1. Popcorns are worked on right side facing rows.

SPECIAL STITCHES

Popcorn (pc): Work 5 dc in same stitch or space indicated, drop loop from hook, insert hook from front to back in first dc made, pull dropped loop through.

CUSHION FRONT

ROW 1: (Right Side) Using Main Color, ch 82, sc in 2nd ch from hook, [sc in next ch] across. (81 sc)

ROW 2: Ch 1, turn, sc in each st across. (81 sc)

ROW 3: Ch 1, turn, sc in first sc, sc in each of next 6 sc, pc (see Special Stitches) in next sc, [sc in each of next 10 sc, pc in next sc] 6 times, sc in each of next 7 sc. (74 sc & 7 popcorns)

ROW 4: Repeat Row 2.

ROW 5: Ch 1, turn, sc in first sc, sc in each of next 5 sc, pc in next sc, sc in next sc, pc in next sc, [sc in each of next 8 sc, pc in next sc, sc in next sc, pc in next sc] 6 times, sc in each of next 6 sc. (67 sc & 14 popcorns)

ROW 6: Repeat Row 2.

ROW 7: Ch 1, turn, sc in first sc, sc in each of next 4 sc, [pc in next sc, sc in next sc] twice, pc in next sc, *sc in each of next 6 sc, [pc in next sc, sc in next sc] twice, pc in next sc; rep from * 5 times more, sc in each of next 5 sc. (60 sc & 21 popcorns)

ROW 8: Repeat Row 2.

ROW 9: Ch 1, turn, sc in first sc, sc in each of next 3 sc, [pc in next sc, sc in next sc] 3 times, pc in next sc, *sc in each of next 4 sc, [pc in next sc, sc in next sc] 3 times, pc in next sc; rep from * 5 times more, sc in each of next 4 sc. (53 sc & 28 popcorns)

ROW 10: Repeat Row 2.

ROW 11: Ch 1, turn, sc in first sc, sc in each of next 2 sc, [pc in next sc, sc in next sc] 4 times, pc in next sc, *sc in each of next 2 sc, [pc in next sc, sc in next sc] 4 times, pc in next sc; rep from * 5 times more, sc in each of next 3 sc. (46 sc & 35 popcorns)

ROW 12: Repeat Row 2.

ROW 13: Repeat Row 9.

ROW 14: Repeat Row 2.

ROW 15: Repeat Row 7.

ROW 16: Repeat Row 2.

ROW 17: Repeat Row 5.

ROW 18: Repeat Row 2.

ROW 19: Repeat Row 3.

ROW 20: Repeat Row 2.

ROW 21-52: Repeat Row 5-20 twice.

ROWS 53: Repeat Row 2. Fasten off and weave in all ends.

ASSEMBLY – Use photo as guide

Using fabric, make a cushion case to cover cushion insert. Insert cushion.

With right side facing, position Cushion Front on cushion case and using needle and thread, tack in place.

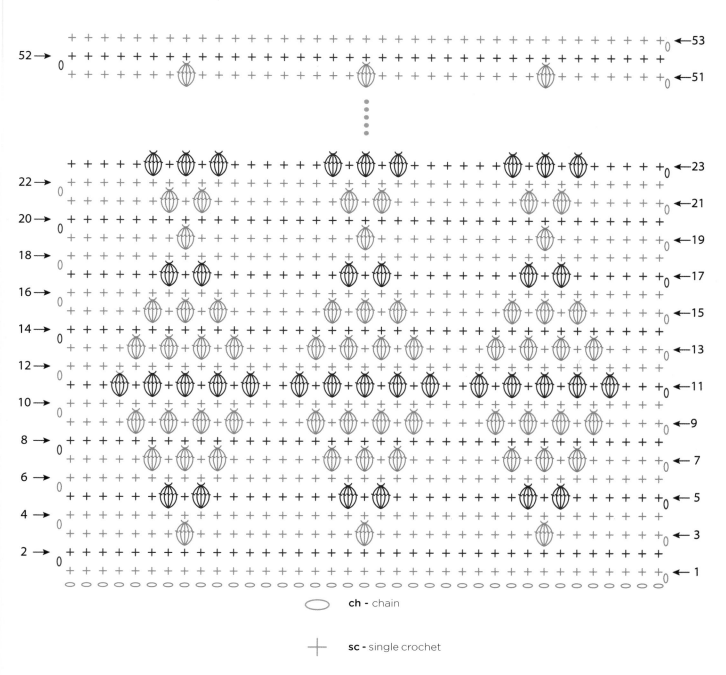

○ **ch -** chain

+ **sc -** single crochet

5-dc popcorn

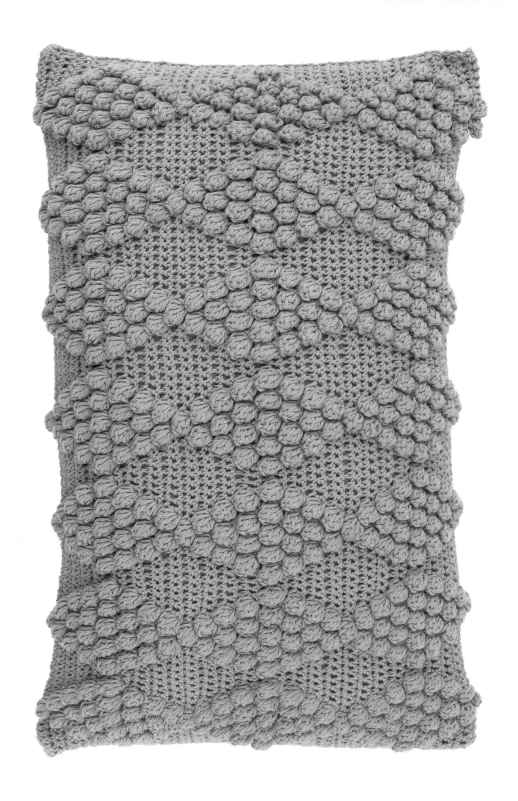

Granny Glass Jar Covers

Glass jars make wonderful storage pots for keeping bits and pieces together around the house. Make pretty crocheted covers for all of them, using colors coordinated with your home décor.

Finished Size

To fit glass jars – about 10" (25 cm) to 12" (30 cm) circumference.

Materials

DMC Natura Just Cotton
Main Color – Lobelia (#82) or Turquoise (#49)

Hook Size D-3 (3.25 mm)

Yarn Needle

Glass Jar

JAR COVER

ROUND 1: Ch 39, taking care not to twist ch, join with sl st to first ch to form ring; ch 3 (counts as first dc, now and throughout), 2 dc in same st as joining, skip next 2 ch, [3 dc in next ch, skip next 2 ch] around; join with sl st to first dc (3ʳᵈ ch of beg ch-3). (13 groups of 3-dc each)

ROUNDS 2-8: Sl st in each of next 2 dc, sl st in sp between dc-groups, ch 3, 2 dc in same sp, [3 dc in next sp between dc-groups] around; join with sl st to first dc (3ʳᵈ ch of beg ch-3). (13 groups of 3-dc each)

At the end of Rnd 8, fasten off and weave in all ends.

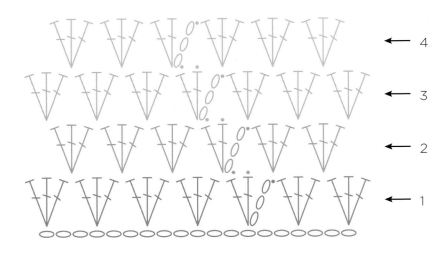

← 4

← 3

← 2

← 1

⬭ **ch -** chain

● **ss -** slip stitch

⊤ **dc -** double crochet

Granny Motif Cushion

This open, lacy floral motif is worked in lovely, pastel shades. Each motif is the same pattern but uses a different colored center give it a pleasing feel while highlighting the lovely texture. Toss it on the sofa or bed to update your interiors!

Finished Size

To fit 16" (40 cm) square cushion.

Each motif measures 5" x 5" (13 cm x 13 cm) after blocking.

Materials

DMC Natura Just Cotton
Main Color – Ibisa (#01)
Color A – Ble (#83)
Color B – Light Green (#12)
Color C – Glicine (#30)
Color D – Gerbera (#98)
Color E – Rose de Meaux (#94)
Color F – Bougainvillea (#93)
Color G – Myosotis (#102)
Color H – Aqua (#100)
Color I – Sichuan (#99)

Hook Size D-3 (3.25 mm)

Yarn Needle
Cushion Insert – 16" (40 cm) square.
Fabric to cover cushion.
Matching thread and needle.

MOTIF – Make 9 (one in each color)

ROUND 1: Using Color, ch 4, join with sl st to first ch to form ring; ch 4 (counts as first dc & ch-1), [dc in ring, ch 1] 7 times; join with sl st to first dc (3rd ch of beg ch-3). (8 dc & 8 ch-1 sps)

ROUND 2: Ch 1, [(sc, ch 3, sc) in next ch-1 sp] around; join with sl st to first sc. (16 sc & 8 ch-3 sps)

ROUND 3: Sl st in next ch-3 sp, ch 3 (counts as first dc, now and throughout), (dc, ch 2, 2 dc) in same sp, [(2 dc, ch 2, 2 dc) in next ch-3 sp] around; join with sl st to first dc (3rd ch of beg ch-3). (32 dc & 8 ch-2 sps)

ROUND 4: Sl st in next dc, sl st in next ch-2 sp, ch 1, (sc, ch 3, sc) in same sp, ch 4, [(sc, ch 3, sc) in next ch-2 sp, ch 4] around; join with sl st to first sc. (16 sc, 8 ch-3 sps & 8 ch-4 sps)

ROUND 5: Sl st in next ch-3 sp, ch 3, (3 dc, ch 1, 4 dc in same sp, sc in next ch-4 sp, [(6 dc, ch 2, 6 dc) in next ch-3 sp, sc in next ch-4 sp, (4 dc, ch 1, 4 dc) in next ch-3 sp, sc in next ch-4 sp] around, ending, (6 dc, ch 2, 6 dc) in next ch-3 sp, sc in next ch-4 sp; join with sl st to first dc (3rd ch of beg ch-3). (4 corner shells, 4 side shells & 8 sc) Fasten off and weave in all ends.

ROUND 6: With right side facing, join Main Color with sl st to first sc on any side, ch 6 (counts as first dc & ch-3), skip next 4 dc, *sc in next ch-1 sp, ch 3, dc in next sc, ch 4, (sc, ch 3, sc) in next corner ch-2 sp, ch 4**, dc in next sc, ch 3; rep from * around, ending at ** on final repeat; join with sl st to first dc (3rd ch of beg ch-6). (8 dc, 12 sc, 12 ch-3 sps & 8 ch-4 lps)

ROUND 7: Ch 3, 3 dc in next ch-3 sp, *4 dc in next ch-3 sp, 5 dc in next ch-4 sp, (3 dc, ch 3, 3 dc) in next corner ch-3 sp, 5 dc in next ch-4 sp**, 4 dc in next ch-3 sp; rep from * around, ending at ** on final repeat; join with sl st to first dc (3rd ch of beg ch-3). (96 dc & 4 corner ch-3 sps) Fasten off and weave in all ends.

MOTIF JOINING

Work the horizontal seams first, and then work the vertical seams. Position and join Motifs to form a three motif by three motif square.

Horizontal Seams

Holding two motifs with wrong sides together (right sides facing), working through both thicknesses and matching stitches, join Main Color with sl st to corner ch-3 sp, ch 1, 2 sc in same sp, *sc in each dc across to next corner, sc in next corner ch-2 sp, holding next two motifs together, 2 sc in corresponding corner ch-3 sp; rep from * once more, sc in each dc across to next corner, 2 sc in last corner ch-2 sp. Fasten off and weave in all ends. Repeat for second horizontal seam.

Vertical Seams

Holding corresponding motifs with wrong sides together (right sides facing), working through both thicknesses and matching stitches, join Main Color with sl st to corner ch-3 sp, ch 1, 2 sc in same sp, *sc in each dc across to next corner, sc in next corner ch-2 sp, ch 1, holding next two motifs together, sc in next corner ch-3 sp; rep from * once more, sc in each dc across to next corner, 2 sc in last corner ch-2 sp. Fasten off and weave in all ends. Repeat for second vertical seam.

BORDER

ROUND 1: With right side of joined Motifs facing, join Main Color with sl st to any outer corner ch-3 sp, ch 1, (sc, ch 1, sc) in same sp, *sc evenly in each dc and sp across to next corner**, (sc, ch 1, sc) in next corner sp; rep from * around, ending at ** on final repeat; join with sl st to first sc.

ROUNDS 2-3: Ch 1, sc in each sc around, working (sc, ch 1, sc) in each corner ch-1 sp; join with sl st to first sc.
At the end of Round 3, fasten off and weave in all ends.

ASSEMBLY – Use photo as guide
Using fabric, sew a pillow case to cover cushion insert. Position motif Square and sew to front of pillow case.

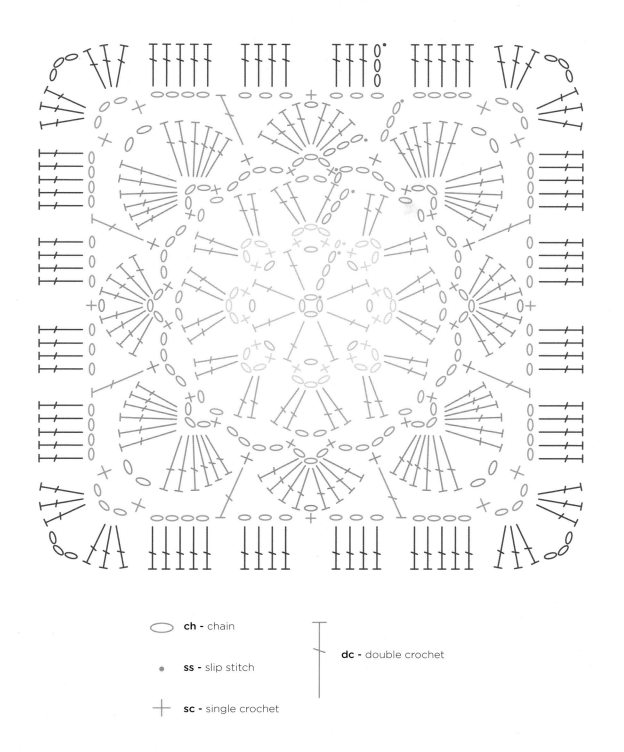

ch - chain

ss - slip stitch

sc - single crochet

dc - double crochet

Granny Square Cushion

Simple and classic, this large granny square pillow is a big trend. Made in bright and zingy colors, it is guaranteed to be loved year after year. The project is super fun and brings a bold injection of vibrant color to any home.

Finished Size

To fit 15" (38 cm) square cushion.

Materials

DMC Natura Just Cotton
Color A – Crimson (#61) 2 balls
Color B – Lobelia (#82) 2 balls
Color C – Turquoise (#49) 2 balls
Color D – Ivory (#02) 2 balls

Hook Size D-3 (3.25 mm)

Yarn Needle
Cushion Insert – 15" (38 cm) square.
Fabric to cover cushion.
Matching thread and needle.

PATTERN NOTES

1. Each color is joined with the right side facing, unless otherwise specified.

2. Fasten off at the end of each Round and weave in all ends, unless otherwise instructed.

3. Color Sequence – *Color A, Color B, Color C, Color D; rep from *.

GRANNY CUSHION

ROUND 1: (Right Side) Starting with Color A, ch 4; join with sl st to first ch to form ring; ch 5 (counts as first dc & ch-2, now and throughout), [3 dc in ring, ch 2] 3 times, 2 dc in ring; join with sl st to first dc (3rd ch of beg ch-5). (12 dc & 4 ch-2 sps) Fasten off Color A and weave in all ends.

ROUND 2: With right side facing, join Color B with sl st to any ch-2 sp, ch 5, 3 dc in same sp, ch 1, [(3 dc, ch 2, 3 dc) in next ch-2 sp, ch 1] around, ending 2 dc in first ch-2 sp; join with sl st to first dc (3rd ch of beg ch-5). (24 dc, 4 ch-1 sps & 4 ch-2 sps) Fasten off Color B and weave in all ends.

ROUND 3: With right side facing, join Color C with sl st to any corner ch-2 sp, ch 5, 3 dc in same sp, ch 1, 3 dc in next ch-1 sp, ch 1, [(3 dc, ch 2, 3 dc) in next ch-2 sp, ch 1, 3 dc in next ch-1 sp, ch 1] around, ending 2 dc in first ch-2 sp; join with sl st to first dc (3rd ch of beg ch-5). (36 dc, 8 ch-1 sps & 4 ch-2 sps) Fasten off Color C and weave in all ends.

ROUNDS 4-28: With right side facing, join next color with sl st to any corner ch-2 sp, ch 5, 3 dc in same sp, *ch 1, [3 dc in next ch-1 sp, ch 1] across to next corner**, (3 dc, ch 2, 3 dc) in next corner ch-2 sp; rep from * around, ending at ** on final repeat, 2 dc in first ch-2 sp; join with sl st to first dc (3rd ch of beg ch-5).
Fasten off and weave in all ends.

ASSEMBLY – Use photo as guide

Cover cushion insert with fabric and sew closed.
Lay Granny square flat, with wrong side facing, and place cushion "on-point" in center, so that each cushion corner touches the middle of the last round. Fold each corner of the granny square downwards so that all four corners meet in the center. Using yarn and needle, sew the sides together. (Or you can sc along the edges.) Fasten off and weave in all ends.

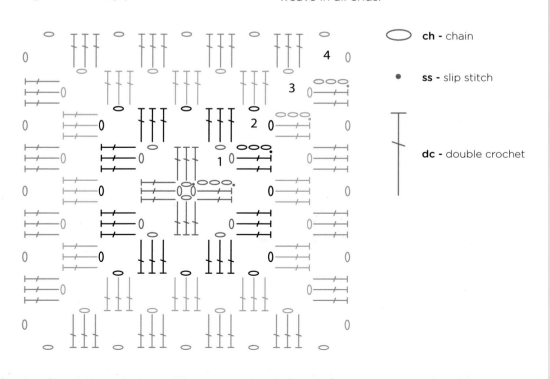

○ **ch -** chain

● **ss -** slip stitch

┬ **dc -** double crochet

Back side of the cushion

75

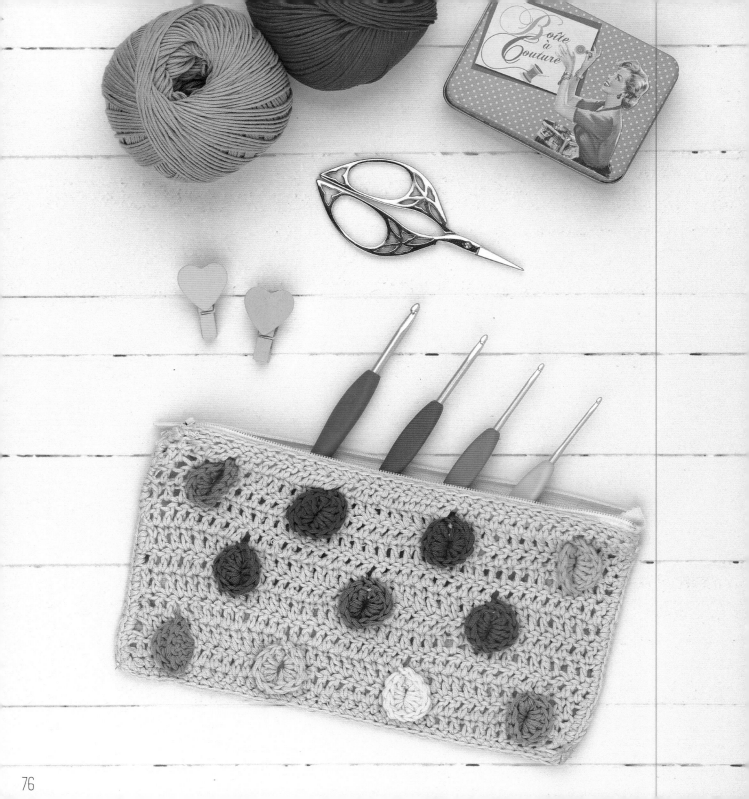

Hook or Pencil Case

Keep your extra-special hooks in an extra-special case!
These pretty cases are great for keeping pencils and other
knick-knacks too. Use eye-popping colors to tailor-make a case
for a special someone.

Finished Size

Hook case measures
about 8 ½" (21.5 cm) wide
by 4 ½" (11.5 cm) long.

Materials

DMC Natura Just Cotton
Main Color – Salomé (#03) 2 balls
Small amounts of the following (for Dots):
Color A - Turquoise (#49)
Color B - Ble (#83)
Color C - Lobelia (#82)
Color D - Pistache (#13)
Color E - Crimson (#61)
Color F - Blue Jeans (#26)
Color G - Siena (#41)
Color H - Giroflee (#85)
Color I - Prune (#59)
Color J - Prussian (#64)
Color K - Coral (#18)

Hook Size D-3 (3.25 mm)

Yarn Needle

Fabric for Case

Needle and matching thread.

Zipper

SPECIAL STITCHES

Dot: Working over 2 dc, join next Color with sl st around post of second dc, ch 3, 5 dc over same dc, rotate piece and work 6 dc over post of first dc; join with sl st to first dc (3rd ch of beg ch-3). Fasten off and weave in ends at back (wrong side) of piece.

FRONT

ROW 1: Using Main Color, ch 43; dc in 4th ch from hook (skipped ch count as first dc), [dc in next ch] across. (40 dc)

ROWS 2-12: Ch 3, turn, [dc in next dc] across. (40 dc) At the end of Row 12, fasten off and weave in all ends.

FINISHING – Use photo as guide

With right side of Front facing, following the Color Sequence for Dots, working in Row 2, *skip first 4 dc, Dot (see Special Stitches) using next 2 dc, [skip next 8 dc, Dot using next 2 dc] 3 times*.

Working in Row 6, skip first 8 dc, Dot using next 2 dc, [skip next 8 dc, Dot using next 2 dc] twice.

Working in Row 10, rep from * to *.

Color Sequence for Dots:

Row 2:	Color A	Row 6:	Color E	Row 10:	Color H
	Color B		Color F		Color I
	Color C		Color G		Color J
	Color D				Color K

ASSEMBLY – Use photo as guide

From the Front measurement, using the Fabric, make and sew a case to size, with a zipper.
With right side of Front facing, position and sew it to the fabric case.

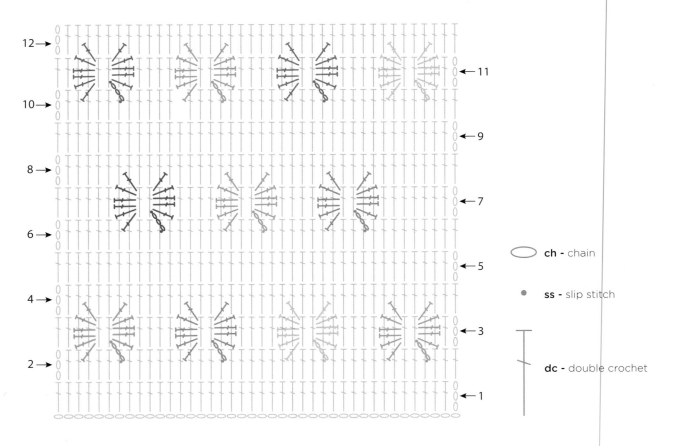

⬭ **ch -** chain

• **ss -** slip stitch

dc - double crochet

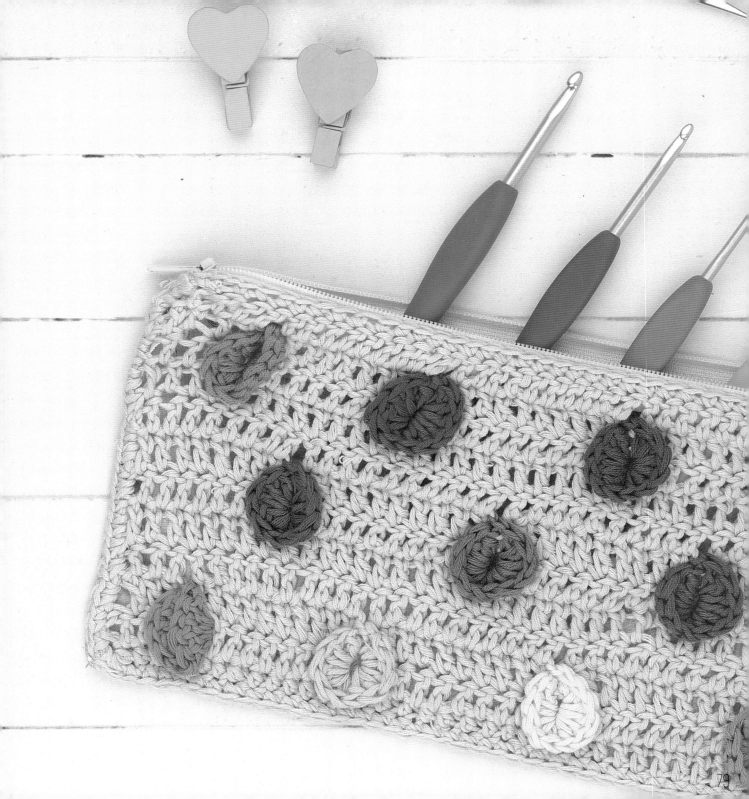

Lacy Blanket

This lacy blanket is light and airy and really soft to touch. The pattern looks complicated, but it is an easy two-row repeat which makes this blanket beautiful. By combining your favorite colors, you can create a one-of-a-kind practical blanket, perfect for snuggling up on chilly evenings.

Finished Size

Blanket measures about 26" (70 cm) wide by 43" (115 cm) long, after blocking.

Materials

DMC Natura Just Cotton
Color A – Amaranto (#33) 4 balls
Color B – Jade (#20) 3 balls
Color C – Siena (#41) 2 balls

Hook Size D-3 (3.25 mm)

Yarn Needle

SPECIAL STITCHES

Two Double Crochet Bobble (2dcbob): Yarn over, insert hook in stitch or space indicated and draw up a loop (3 loops on hook), yarn over, pull through 2 loops on hook (2 loops on remain on hook), yarn over, insert hook in same stitch or space and draw up a loop (4 loops on hook), yarn over, pull through 2 loops on hook (3 loops on hook), yarn over, pull through all 3 loops on hook.

BLANKET

ROW1: (Right Side) Starting with Color A, ch152, (2 hdc, ch2, 2 hdc) in 5th ch from hook (skipped ch count as first hdc & 2 skipped chs), [skip next 2 ch, 2dcbob (see Special Stitches) in next ch, skip next 2 ch, (2 hdc, ch 2, 2 hdc) in next ch] across, ending skip next 2 ch, hdc in last ch. (24 shells, 23 bobs & 2 hdc)

ROW 2: Ch 2 (counts as first hdc, now and throughout), turn, (2 sc, ch 2, 2 sc) in first ch-2 sp, [sc in next 2dcbob, (2 sc, ch 2, 2 sc) in next ch-2 sp] across, ending with hdc in last hdc. (24 shells, 23 sc & 2 hdc)

ROW 3: Ch 2, turn, (2 hdc, ch 2, 2 hdc) in first ch-2 sp, [2dcbob in next sc, (2 hdc, ch 2, 2 hdc) in next ch-2 sp] across, ending hdc in last hdc. (24 shells, 23 bobs & 2 hdc)

Repeat Rows 2-3, until Blanket measures 25" (65 cm) from beginning, ending on Row 3 and changing to Color B in last hdc.

With Color B, repeat Rows 2-3 until Blanket measures 36" (98 cm) from beginning, ending on Row 3 and changing to Color C in last hdc.

With Color C, repeat Rows 2-3 until Blanket measures 43" (110 cm) from beginning, ending on Row 2. Fasten off and weave in all ends.

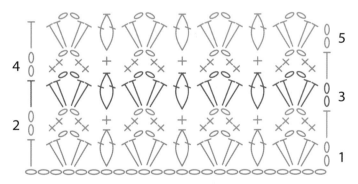

⬭ **ch -** chain

+ **sc -** single crochet

⊤ **hdc -** half double crochet

◇ **2-dc bobble**

Lemon Slice Rug

When life gives you lemons, make a rug! This citrus-wonder is quickly made up using super-chunky cotton yarn and a large hook. It is super soft and modern and will definitely add some zing to your personal space.

Finished Size

Rug measures 35 ½" (90 cm) wide
and 15 ½" (40 cm) long.

Materials

DMC Natura Just Cotton XL
Color A – White (#01) 2 balls
Color B – Yellow (#09) 4 balls

Hook Size L-11 (8.00 mm)

Yarn Needle

RUG

ROW 1: (Wrong Side) Starting with Color A, ch 3; join with sl st to first ch to form ring; ch 2 (counts as first hdc, now and throughout), 4 hdc in ring. DO NOT JOIN. (5 hdc)

ROW 2: Ch 2, turn, hdc in first hdc, [2 hdc in next hdc] across. (10 hdc)

ROW 3: Ch 2, turn, 2 hdc in next hdc, [hdc in next hdc, 2 hdc in next hdc] across. (15 hdc)

ROW 4: Ch 2, turn, hdc in next hdc, 2 hdc in next hdc, [hdc in each of next 2 hdc, 2 hdc in next hdc] across. (20 hdc)

ROW 5: Ch 2, turn, hdc in each of next 2 hdc, 2 hdc in next hdc, [hdc in each of next 3 hdc, 2 hdc in next hdc] across. (25 hdc) Fasten off Color A and weave in all ends.

ROW 6: Turn (wrong side facing), join Color B with sl st to first hdc, ch 2, hdc in each of next 3 hdc, 2 hdc in next hdc, [hdc in each of next 4 hdc, 2 hdc in next hdc] across. (30 hdc)

ROW 7: Ch 2, turn, hdc in each of next 4 hdc, 2 hdc in next hdc, [hdc in each of next 5 hdc, 2 hdc in next hdc] across. (35 hdc)

ROW 8: Ch 2, turn, hdc in each of next 5 hdc, 2 hdc in next hdc, [hdc in each of next 6 hdc, 2 hdc in next hdc] across. (40 hdc)

ROW 9: Ch 2, turn, hdc in each of next 6 hdc, 2 hdc in next hdc, [hdc in each of next 7 hdc, 2 hdc in next hdc] across. (45 hdc)

ROW 10: Ch 2, turn, hdc in each of next 7 hdc, 2 hdc in next hdc, [hdc in each of next 8 hdc, 2 hdc in next hdc] across. (50 hdc)

ROW 11: Ch 2, turn, hdc in each of next 8 hdc, 2 hdc in next hdc, [hdc in each of next 9 hdc, 2 hdc in next hdc] across. (55 hdc)

ROW 12: Ch 2, turn, hdc in each of next 9 hdc, 2 hdc in next hdc, [hdc in each of next 10 hdc, 2 hdc in next hdc] across. (60 hdc)

ROW 13: Ch 2, turn, hdc in each of next 10 hdc, 2 hdc in next hdc, [hdc in each of next 11 hdc, 2 hdc in next hdc] across. (65 hdc)

ROW 14: Ch 2, turn, hdc in each of next 11 hdc, 2 hdc in next hdc, [hdc in each of next 12 hdc, 2 hdc in next hdc] across. (70 hdc)

ROW 15: Ch 2, turn, hdc in each of next 12 hdc, 2 hdc in next hdc, [hdc in each of next 13 hdc, 2 hdc in next hdc] across. (75 hdc)

ROW 16: Ch 2, turn, hdc in each of next 13 hdc, 2 hdc in next hdc, [hdc in each of next 14 hdc, 2 hdc in next hdc] across. (80 hdc)

ROW 17: Ch 2, turn, hdc in each of next 14 hdc, 2 hdc in next hdc, [hdc in each of next 15 hdc, 2 hdc in next hdc] across. (85 hdc)

ROW 18: Ch 2, turn, hdc in each of next 15 hdc, 2 hdc in next hdc, [hdc in each of next 16 hdc, 2 hdc in next hdc] across. (90 hdc)

ROW 19: Ch 2, turn, hdc in each of next 16 hdc, 2 hdc in next hdc, [hdc in each of next 17 hdc, 2 hdc in next hdc] across. (95 hdc)

ROW 20: Ch 2, turn, hdc in each of next 17 hdc, 2 hdc in next hdc, [hdc in each of next 18 hdc, 2 hdc in next hdc] across. (100 hdc)

ROW 21: Ch 2, turn, hdc in each of next 18 hdc, 2 hdc in next hdc, [hdc in each of next 19 hdc, 2 hdc in next hdc] across. (105 hdc)

ROW 22: Ch 2, turn, hdc in each of next 19 hdc, 2 hdc in next hdc, [hdc in each of next 20 hdc, 2 hdc in next hdc] across. (110 hdc)

ROW 23: Ch 2, turn, hdc in each of next 20 hdc, 2 hdc in next hdc, [hdc in each of next 21 hdc, 2 hdc in next hdc] across. (115 hdc) Fasten off Color B and weave in all ends.

ROW 24: Turn (wrong side facing), join Color A with sl st to first hdc, ch 2, hdc in each of next 21 hdc, 2 hdc in next hdc, [hdc in each of next 22 hdc, 2 hdc in next hdc] across. (120 hdc)

ROW 25: Ch 2, turn, hdc in each of next 22 hdc, 2 hdc in next hdc, [hdc in each of next 23 hdc, 2 hdc in next hdc] across. (125 hdc) Fasten off Color A and weave in all ends.

ROW 26: Turn (wrong side facing), join Color B with sl st to first hdc, ch 2, [hdc in next hdc] across. (125 hdc)

ROWS 27-28: Ch 2, turn, [hdc in next hdc] across. (125 hdc) At the end of Row 28, fasten off Color B and weave in all ends.

WEDGES (using Surface Stitches)

Surface Stitches

Make a slip knot. Insert hook from front (right side) to back (wrong side) through indicated stitch. Place slip knot on hook (at back) and pull hook to the front, keeping knot at the back.

*Insert hook in corresponding stitch on next row, pull up yarn through fabric and loop on hook (slip stitch made); repeat from * across.

With Color A, create lines from Row 5 to Row 24 using Surface Stitches, fastening off after each line and weaving in ends.

First line – from 5th stitch on Row 5 to 24th stitch on Row 24.
Second line – from 10th stitch on Row 5 to 48th stitch on Row 24.
Third line – from 15th stitch on Row 5 to 72nd stitch on Row 24.
Fourth – from 20th stitch on Row 5 to 96th stitch on Row 24.

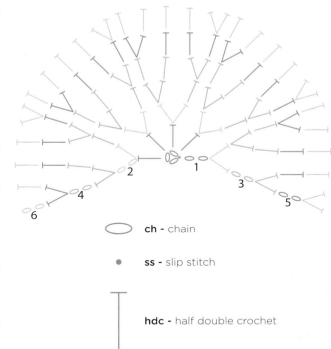

ch - chain

ss - slip stitch

hdc - half double crochet

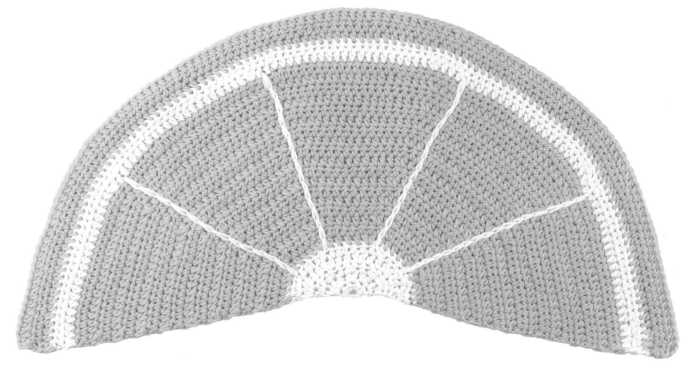

Vintage Cushion Cover

This sweet, pastel doily makes a wonderful cushion cover, reminiscent of the "good old days". Each round is worked up in a different stitch and in a different color. You can choose your own color palette to fit in with your home décor, or make it up using colors of left-over yarn - a true stash-buster.

Finished Size

About 15 ½" (40 cm) diameter.

Materials

DMC Natura Just Cotton

Color A – Ble (#83)   2 balls
Color B – Rose Soraya (#32) 1 ball
Color C – Turquoise (#49) 1 ball
Color D – Ibisa (#01)   1 ball

Hook Size D-3 (3.25 mm)

Yarn Needle
Round Cushion Insert (15 ¾" (40 cm)
Fabric for Cushion (optional)
Needle & Thread (optional)

ROUND 18: Join Color B with sl st to any sc, beg-3dcbob in same st as joining, ch 2, skip next sc, [3dcbob in next sc, ch 2, skip next sc] around; join with sl st to top of first 3dcbob. (82 bobbles & 82 ch-2 sps)

ROUND 19: Join Color C with sl st to any ch-2 sp, ch 7 (counts as first tr & ch 3), tr in same sp, skip next ch-1 sp, [(tr, ch 3, tr) in next ch-2 sp, skip next ch-2 sp] around; join with sl st to first tr (4th ch of beg ch-7). (82 tr & 41 ch-3 sps)

ROUND 20: Join Color D with sl st to any ch-3 sp, ch 3, 5 dc in same sp, [6 dc in next ch-3 sp] around; join with sl st to first dc (3rd ch of beg ch-3). (246 dc)

ROUND 21: Using Color A, join with sc to any dc, [sc in next dc] around; join with sl st to first sc. (246 sc)

ROUND 22: Join Color B with sl st to any sc, ch 2, (hdc, ch 1, hdc) in same st as joining, skip next 2 sc, [(hdc, ch 1, hdc) in next sc, skip next 2 sc] around; join with sl st to first hdc. (164 hdc & 82 ch-1 sps)

ROUND 23: Join Color C with sl st to any ch-1 sp, ch 3, 2 dc in same sp, [3 dc in next ch-1 sp] around; join with sl st to first dc (3rd ch of beg ch-3). (82 groups of 3-dc each)

ROUND 24: Join Color D with sl st to sp between dc-groups, ch 3, dc in same sp, [2 dc in sp between next dc-group] around; join with sl st to first dc (3rd ch of beg ch-3). (82 groups of 2-dc each) DO NOT FASTEN OFF.

ASSEMBLY – Use photo as guide

If desired, cover cushion insert with fabric and sew in place.

JOINING & BORDER

ROUND 1: With right sides of Front and Back facing (wrong sides together) and Front facing, continuing with Color D, working through both thicknesses, ch 1, sc in same dc as joining, matching stitches, [sc in next dc] around, inserting cushion form before closing; join with sl st to first sc. (164 sc) Fasten off Color D and weave in all ends.

ROUND 2: Using Color B, join with sc to any sc, ch 3, skip next sc, [sc in next sc, ch 3, skip next sc] around; join with sl st to first sc. (82 ch-3 sps) DO NOT FASTEN OFF.

ROUND 3: Sl st in next ch-3 sp, ch 3, 7 dc in same sp, sc in next ch-3 sp, [8 dc in next ch-3 sp, sc in next ch-3 sp] around; join with sl st to first dc (3rd ch of beg ch-3). Fasten off and weave in all ends.

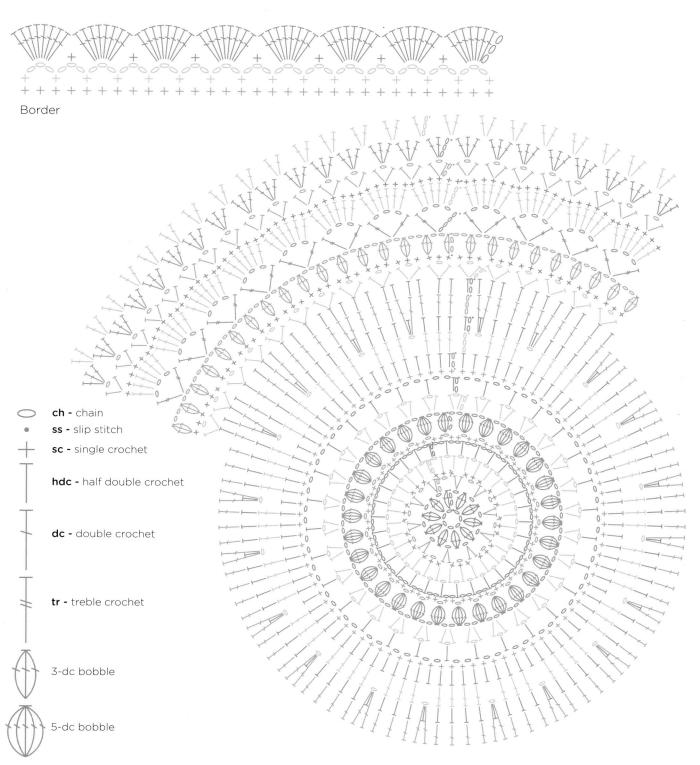

Border

ch - chain

ss - slip stitch

sc - single crochet

hdc - half double crochet

dc - double crochet

tr - treble crochet

3-dc bobble

5-dc bobble

93

Elegant Purse

This cute, textured purse is a great accessory for bringing out your girly side. It's simple to make and perfect as a last-minute present. The stitch pattern is great and suitable for beginners.

Finished Size

Purse measures 7" (18 cm) long and 5" (13 cm) high.

Materials

DMC Natura Just Cotton Medium
Main Color – Pink (#444)   3 balls

Hook Size G-6 (4.00 mm)

Yarn Needle

Link Chain – about 45" (115 cm) long.

Magnetic Snap Pin.

PURSE

ROW 1: (Right Side) Using Main Color, ch 91; sl st in 3rd ch from hook (skipped 2-chs count as first hdc), [hdc in next ch, sl st in next ch] across. (45 hdc & 45 sl sts) Mark the ch that the last sl st was worked in.

ROW 2: Ch 2 (counts as first hdc, now and throughout), turn, [sl st in next hdc, hdc in next sl st] across, ending with sl st in top of last hdc (2nd ch of skipped chs). (45 hdc & 45 sl sts)

ROW 3: Ch 2, turn, sl st in next hdc, hdc in next sl st] across, ending with sl st in top of last hdc (2nd ch of ch-2). (45 hdc & 45 sl sts)

ROWS 4-17: Repeat Row 3.
At the end of Row 17, piece should measure 7" (17.5 cm) from beginning, ending on a right side row. Mark the last sl st made on last row. Fasten off and weave in all ends.

GUSSET PIECES (Make 2)

ROW 1: (Right Side) Using Main Color, ch 17; sc in 2nd ch from hook, [sc in next ch] across. (16 sc)

ROWS 2-21: Ch 1, turn, sc in each sc across. (16 sc)
At the end of Row 21, Gusset should measure 4 ½" (11.5 cm) from beginning, ending on a right side row. Finish off leaving long end for sewing.

ASSEMBLY – Use photo /diagram as guide

Using long ends and yarn needle, sew three sides of Gusset (not the last row) to long side (first row) of Purse, starting at marked stitch and easing in around corners. There will be about 35 sts left unsewn on Purse. This forms the flap. Do not finish off.

Pinch the ends of the last row of the Gusset together (towards the wrong side of purse), and tack to secure. (The chain is attached at this pinched point.) Sew across last row. Finish off and weave in ends.

Repeat with other Gusset sewing along last row of Purse, and ending in line with the first Gusset.

Attach the chain to each side of the Gusset.

Fold flap over and sew or glue magnetic pin to the front and front flap.

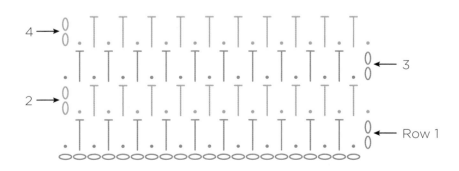

○ **ch -** chain

● **ss -** slip stitch

T **hdc -** half double crochet

Spiral Coasters

Mix and match colors to create vibrant two-toned coasters. They're easy to make and a fun project for beginners. Grab your hook and yarn and start spiralling!

Finished Size

Each Coaster – About 4 ½" (11.5 cm) across.

Materials

DMC Natura Just Cotton
Color A – Safran (#47)
Color B – Prussian (#64)

Hook Size D-3 (3.25 mm)

Yarn Needle

Stitch markers

SPECIAL STITCHES

Join With Single Crochet (join with sc) - With slip knot on hook, insert hook into stitch or space indicated and pull up a loop (2 loops on hook). Yarn over and pull through both loops on hook (first single crochet made).

COASTER

ROUND 1: (Right Side) Starting with Color A, ch 3; join with sl st to first ch to form ring; ch 1, (2 sc, 2 hdc, 2 dc) in ring; remove hook and place stitch marker in loop; using Color B, join with sc (see Special Stitches) to ring (next to last dc made), (sc, 2 hdc, 2 dc) in ring. DO NOT JOIN. (12 sts – 4 sc, 4 hdc & 4 dc)

ROUND 2: Continuing with Color B (working in Color A sts), *2 dc in each of next 2 sc, 2 dc in each of next 2 hdc, 2 dc in each of next dc*; remove hook and place stitch marker in loop; pick up Color A; (working in Color B sts), rep from * to * once. (24 dc – 12 dc in each color)

ROUND 3: Continuing with Color A, *[dc in next dc, 2 dc in next dc] 6 times*, remove hook and place stitch marker in loop; pick up Color B; rep from * to * once. (36 dc – 18 dc in each color)

ROUND 4: Continuing with Color B, *[dc in each of next 2 dc, 2 dc in next dc] 6 times*, remove hook and place stitch marker in loop; pick up Color A; rep from * to * once. (48 dc – 24 dc in each color)

⬭	**ch -** chain
•	**ss -** slip stitch
+	**sc -** single crochet
⊤	**hdc -** half double crochet
⊥	**dc -** double crochet

ROUND 5: Continuing with Color A, *[dc in each of next 3 dc, 2 dc in next dc] 6 times*, remove hook and place stitch marker in loop; pick up Color B; rep from * to * once. (60 dc – 30 dc in each color)

ROW 6: Continuing with Color B, [dc in each of next 4 dc, 2 dc in next dc] 6 times, remove hook and place stitch marker in loop; pick up Color A; hdc in each of next 2 dc, sc in each of next 2 dc, sl st in next dc; fasten off Color A. Pick up Color B, dc in next hdc, hdc in each of next 2 sts, sc in each of next 2 sts, sl st in next dc. Fasten off Color B and weave in all ends.

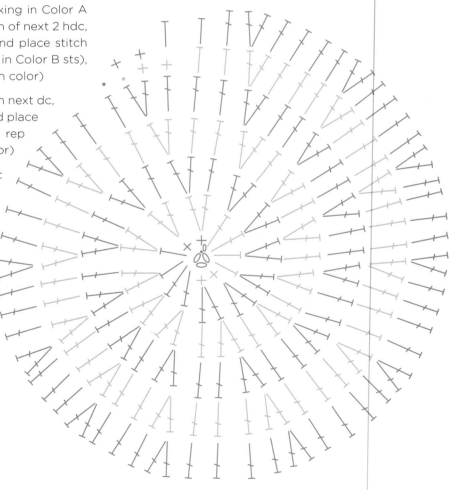

Stool Cover

No frills nor fuss. Just some hooky-goodness in a good, practical stool cover. The beauty of this cover is the simplicity of its design. It's worked up in a spiral using alternating and contrasting colors.

Finished Size

Cover measures 13 ½" (35 cm) diameter and 4" (10 cm) high.

MATERIALS

DMC Natura Just Cotton Medium
Color A – Pink (#444) 4 balls
Color B – Denim Blue (#77) 4 balls

Hook Size G-6 (4.00 mm)

Yarn Needle

Stool with seat diameter of 13 ½" (35 cm).
(IKEA Frosta Stool used in the photo)

PATTERN NOTES

The design is worked in a spiral.
Color changes are worked in the last stitch before new color is needed.

Options for working:

1. You can leave the unused yarn hanging to the back of the work, and pick it up when needed, creating long strands on the wrong side. (Take care not to pull the strands too tight when joining, or leave them too loose so the stitches get loose.)

2. Work over unused color until it is needed. (This creates a thicker fabric and the unused color can be seen through the stitches.)

3. A happy medium is to 'catch' the unused yarn (by working over it) every 3-4 stitches, creating shorter strands on the wrong side.

STOOL COVER

ROUND 1: (Right Side) Starting with Color A, ch 4; join with sl st to first ch to form ring; ch 1, sc in ring, 7 hdc in ring. (8 sts) DO NOT JOIN.

ROUND 2: 2 hdc in next sc, changing color to Color B in last hdc, with Color B, 2 hdc in next hdc, *changing to Color A in last hdc, with Color A, 2 hdc in next hdc, changing to Color B in last hdc, with Color B, 2 hdc in next hdc; rep from * twice more, picking up Color A in last hdc. (16 hdc)

ROUND 3: *With Color A, hdc in next hdc, 2 hdc in next hdc, changing to Color B in last hdc, with Color B, hdc in next hdc, 2 hdc in next hdc, changing to Color A in last hdc; rep from * 3 times more. (24 hdc)

ROUND 4: *With Color A, hdc in each of next 2 hdc, 2 hdc in next hdc, changing to Color B in last hdc, with Color B, hdc in each of next 2 hdc, 2 hdc in next hdc, changing to Color A in last hdc; rep from * 3 times more. (32 hdc)

ROUND 5: *With Color A, hdc in each of next 3 hdc, 2 hdc in next hdc, changing to Color B in last hdc, with Color B, hdc in each of next 3 hdc, 2 hdc in next hdc, changing

to Color A in last hdc; rep from * 3 times more. (40 hdc)

ROUND 6: *With Color A, hdc in each of next 4 hdc, 2 hdc in next hdc, changing to Color B in last hdc, with Color B, hdc in each of next 4 hdc, 2 hdc in next hdc, changing to Color A in last hdc; rep from * 3 times more. (48 hdc)

ROUNDS 7-19: Continue as established, increasing 8 sts per round (1 increase per color change). At the end of Rnd 19, there are 152 sts (19 sts per color change).

ROUNDS 20-22: *With Color A, hdc in each of next 19 hdc, changing to Color B in last hdc, with Color B, hdc in each of next 19 hdc, changing to Color A in last hdc; rep from * 3 times more. (152 hdc)

ROUND 23: *With Color A, sc in each of next 19 hdc, changing to Color B in last sc, with Color B, sc in each of next 19 hdc, changing to Color A in last sc; rep from * 3 times more, sl st in next sc. (152 sc) Fasten off and weave in all ends.

FINISHING – Use photo as guide
Weave a separate strand of yarn through last round of stitches. Place Cover on stool and tug yarn ends gently to prevent Cover slipping off Stool. Tie ends in a knot.

ch - chain

ss - slip stitch

sc - single crochet

hdc - half double crochet

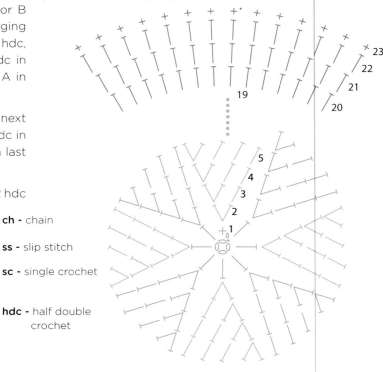

Teapot Cover

Many of us need an early morning cuppa to kick-start the day. Make sure your tea is piping hot with this charming crocheted teapot cover. Featuring a lovely textured shell-stitch pattern, it will definitely jazz up your breakfast table. A drawstring top means it can be adjusted to custom-fit any teapot.

Finished Size

Teapot Cover – about 8" (20 cm) long and 6 ½" (16.5 cm) wide.
To fit standard teapot - approximately 6" (15 cm) tall, with 6" (15 cm) diameter.

Materials

DMC Natura Just Cotton
Main Color – Star Light (#27) 2 balls

Small amounts of:
Color A – Tournesol (#16)
Color B – Crimson (#61)
Color C – Pistache (#13)

Hook Size D-3 (3.25 mm)

Yarn Needle

COVER SIDES (Make 2)

ROW 1: (Right Side) Using Main Color, ch 38; sc in 2nd ch from hook, [skip next 2 ch, 5 dc in next ch, skip next 2 ch, sc in next ch] across. (6 shells & 7 sc)

ROW 2: Ch 3, turn, 2 dc in first sc, [skip next 2 dc, sc in next (center) dc, skip next 2 dc, 5 dc in next sc] across, ending skip next 2 dc, sc in next (center) dc, skip next 2 dc, 3 dc in last sc. (5 shells, 2 half-shells & 6 sc)

ROW 3: Ch 1, turn, sc in first dc, [skip next 2 dc, 5 dc in next sc, skip next 2 dc, sc in next dc] across. (6 shells & 7 sc)

Repeat Rows 2-3 until piece measures 8" (20 cm) from beginning. Fasten off and weave in all ends.

ASSEMBLY – Use photo as guide

With right sides of both Cover Sides facing (wrong sides together), using needle and yarn, sew pieces together, leaving a gap on each side for the spout and handle of teapot.

CORD

Using Main Color, ch 95; sc in 2nd ch from hook, [sc in next ch] across. Fasten off and weave in all ends. Weave Cord through shell stitches about 5-6 rows from top.

FLOWER (Make 2)

ROUND 1: (Right Side) Using Color A, ch 3; join with sl st to first ch to form ring; ch 1, 5 sc in ring; join with sl st to first sc. Fasten off and weave in all ends.

ROUND 2: With right side facing, join Color B with sl st to any sc, [ch 5, sl st in next sc] around. (5 petals) Finish off leaving long end for sewing.

LEAVES (Make 2)

ROW 1: (Right Side) Using Color C, ch 8, sc in 2nd ch from hook, hdc in next ch, dc in each of next 3 ch, hdc in next ch, (sc, sl st) in last ch. Finish off leaving long end for sewing.

FINISHING – Use photo as guide

Using long ends and yarn needle, sew Flowers and leaves to front of Teapot Cover.

Leaf

Flower

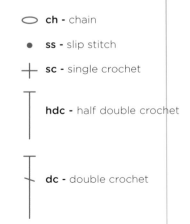

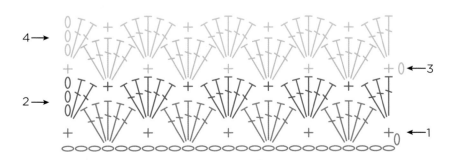

◯ **ch** - chain

● **ss** - slip stitch

✛ **sc** - single crochet

hdc - half double crochet

dc - double crochet

Tissue Box Cover

Conceal your tissue box beneath a highly-textured cover made with vibrant colors. It's easy to make and looks really impressive. Make yours in any color combination to add your special touch.

Finished Size

To fit standard tissue box measuring 4 ½" (11.5 cm) wide, 8 ½" (21.5 cm) long and 3" (7.5 cm) high.

Materials

DMC Natura Just Cotton
Color A – Giroflee (#85) 2 balls
Color B – Pistache (#13) 1 balls
Color C – Bamboo (#76) 1 balls

Hook: Size G-6 (4.00 mm)

Yarn Needle

PATTERN NOTES

1. Each row is worked in a new color and the new color is joined in the last stitch of the previous row, unless otherwise specified.

2. Each round is worked in a new color. The new color is joined each round.

3. Fasten off at the end of each row/round (unless otherwise instructed) and weave in all ends.

SPECIAL STITCHES

Join With Single Crochet (join with sc) - With slip knot on hook, insert hook into stitch or space indicated and pull up a loop (2 loops on hook). Yarn over and pull through both loops on hook (first single crochet made).

TOP OF COVER

Color Sequence: *Color A, Color B, Color A, Color C; rep from *.

ROW 1: (Right Side) Starting with Color A, ch 44, sc in 4th ch from hook (skipped ch count as first turning ch-2 sp), [ch 1, skip next ch, sc in next ch] across, changing to Color B in last sc. (21 sc, 20 ch-1 sps & 1 ch-2 sp) Fasten off Color A and weave in all ends.

ROW 2: With new color, ch 2, turn, skip first sc, [sc in next ch-1 sp, ch 1] across, ending with sc in last ch-2 sp, changing color to next color. (21 sc, 20 ch-1 sps & 1 ch-2 sp)

ROWS 3-12: Following color sequence, repeat Row 2.

ROW 13: With new color, ch 2, turn, skip first sc, sc in next ch-1 sp, [ch 1, sc in next ch-1 sp] 4 times, ch 21, skip next 11 sc (& 10 ch-1 sps), [sc in next ch-1 sp, ch 1] across, ending

⬯ **ch** - chain   + **sc** - single crochet

with sc in last ch-2 sp, changing color to next color. (11 sc, 9 ch-1 sps, ch-21 lp & 1 ch-2 sp)

ROW 14: With new color, ch 2, turn, skip first sc, sc in next ch-1 sp, [ch 1, sc in next ch-1 sp] 4 times, ch 1, skip next sc, sc in next ch, [ch 1, skip next ch, sc in next ch] 10 times, ch 1, [sc in next ch-1 sp, ch 1] across, ending with sc in last ch-2 sp, changing color to next color. (21 sc, 20 ch-1 sps & 1 ch-2 sp)

ROWS 15-25: Repeat Row 2. At the end of Row 25, change to the next color in sequence.

BOX SIDES

ROUND 1: Using next color, ch 2, turn (right side facing), skip first sc, [sc in next ch-1 sp, ch 1] across, ending with (sc, ch 1, sc) in last ch-2 sp, *working in sides of rows, [ch 1, skip next row, sc in ch-2 sp of next row] across*, ch 1, working in unused lps on other side of starting ch, (sc, ch 1, sc) in first ch, [ch 1, skip next ch, sc in next ch] across, ending with ch 1, (sc, ch 1, sc) in corner ch-2 sp; repeat from * to *, ch 1, (sc, ch 1, sc) in last ch-2 sp; join with sl st to first sc. Fasten off and weave in all ends.

ROUND 2: Turn, using next Color, join with sc (see Special Stitches) to any ch-1 sp, ch 1, [sc in next ch-1 sp, ch 1] around; join with sl st to first sc. Fasten off and weave in all ends.

ROUNDS 3-20: Repeat Round 2, ending with Color A. At the end of Round 20, fasten off and weave in all ends.

Tunisian Tote Bag

This is the perfect project to practice your Tunisian crochet. It is an easy, yet elegant, tote bag, which is roomy enough for holding your WIPs (Works In Progress). It can also be used as a green shopping bag. Embellished with leather handles, it will definitely become your go-to handbag.

Finished Size

Tote measures about 11 ½" (29 cm) wide and 14" (35.5 cm) high.

Materials

DMC Natura Just Cotton Medium
Main Color – Rust Orange (#109)   5 balls

Hook Size I-9 (5.50 mm) & Tunisian Hook Size I-9 (5.50 mm)

Yarn Needle

Set of Leather Handles

PATTERN NOTES

Tunisian Crochet

Tunisian Simple Stitch (TSS) is easy to learn. It is worked right side facing and you never turn your work.

Each row of Tunisian Crochet consists of two passes. A Forward Pass, in which you pick up loops onto your long hook; and a Return Pass, where you work off the loops.

TOTE BASE

ROUND 1: Using normal hook and Main Color, ch 38, 3 sc in 2nd ch from hook, 2 sc in next ch, sc in each of next 33 ch, 2 sc in next ch, 3 sc in last ch, working in unused lps on other side of starting ch, 2 sc in next ch, sc in each of next 33 ch, 2 sc in next ch; join with sl st to first sc. (80 sc)

ROUND 2: Ch 1, 2 sc in same st as joining, 2 sc in each of next 3 sc, sc in each of next 35 sc, 2 sc in each of next 5 sc, sc in each of next 35 sc, 2 sc in last sc; join with sl st to first sc. (90 sc)

ROUNDS 3-4: Ch 1, sc in same st as joining, [sc in next sc] around; join with sl st to first sc. (90 sc)

At the end of Round 4, Fasten off and weave in all ends.

TOTE SIDES

BASE ROW: (Right Side) Using Main Color and Tunisian hook, ch 90.

Forward Pass: Pick up loop in 2nd ch from hook, leaving loops on hook, pick up loop in each ch across. (90 lps on hook)

Return Pass: Ch 1, *yo, draw through 2 lps on hook; rep from * across to end (1 lp remains on hook).

TUNISIAN SIMPLE STITCH (TSS) ROW:

Forward Pass: Insert hook from right to left under 2nd vertical bar of stitch (skip the first one, which is directly below the loop on your hook), yarn over hook and pull loop through (two loops on hook), keeping all loops on hook, *insert hook under next vertical bar and pull up a loop; rep from * across to last stitch, insert hook

through two loops of last st (the front lp and back ridge of the ch-st) and pick up loop. (90 lps on hook)

Return Pass: Ch 1, *yo, draw through 2 lps on hook; rep from * across to end.

Repeat the TSS row until piece measures nearly 14" (35.5 cm) from beginning.

Last Row (Bind Off)

Forward Pass Only: *Insert hook from right to left under 2nd vertical bar and pick up lp, pulling it through the loop on hook (a slip stitch – leaving 1 lp on hook); rep from * across. No Return Pass. Fasten off and weave in all ends.

ASSEMBLY – Use photo as guide

With right side facing, fold Tote Sides in half and using needle and yarn, sew Base Row to Last Row, to form a tube. Position and sew Tote Base around one opening of tube. Position and sew Handles on either side at top of Tote.

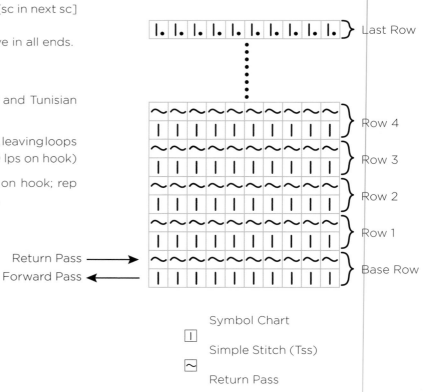

Last Row

Row 4

Row 3

Row 2

Row 1

Base Row

Return Pass →
Forward Pass ←

Symbol Chart

| Simple Stitch (Tss)

~ Return Pass

Crochet Basics

SLIP KNOT

Almost every crochet project starts with a slip knot on the hook. This is not mentioned in any pattern – it is assumed.

To make a slip knot, form a loop with your yarn (the tail end hanging behind your loop); insert the hook through the loop, and pick up the ball end of the yarn. Draw yarn through loop. Keeping loop on hook, gently tug the tail end to tighten the knot. Tugging the ball end tightens the loop.

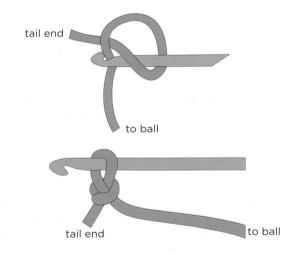

YARN OVER (yo)

This is a common practice, especially with the taller stitches.

With a loop on your hook, wrap the yarn (attached to the ball) from back to front around the shaft of your hook.

CHAIN STITCH (ch)

The chain stitch is the foundation of most crochet projects.

The foundation chain is a series of chain stitches in which you work the first row of stitches.

To make a chain stitch, you start with a slip knot (or loop) on the hook. Yarn over and pull the yarn through the loop on your hook (first chain stitch made). For more chain stitches, repeat: Yarn over, pull through loop on hook.

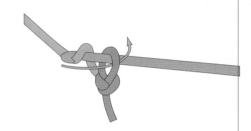

Hint: Don't pull the stitches too tight, otherwise they will be difficult to work in.

When counting chain stitches, do not count the slip knot, nor the loop on the hook. Only count the number of 'v's.

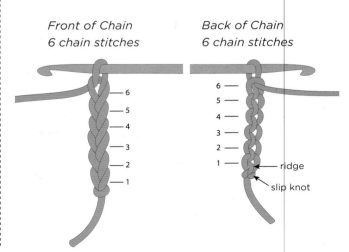

Front of Chain
6 chain stitches

Back of Chain
6 chain stitches

SLIP STITCH (sl st)

Starting with a loop on your hook, insert hook in stitch or space specified and pull up a loop, pulling it through the loop on your hook as well.

The slip stitch is commonly used to attach new yarn and to join rounds.

Attaching a New Color or New Ball of Yarn (or Joining with a Slip Stitch (join with sl st)).

Make a slip knot with the new color (or yarn) and place loop on hook. Insert hook from front to back in the (usually) first stitch (unless specified otherwise). Yarn over and pull loop through stitch and loop on hook (slip stitch made).

SINGLE CROCHET (sc)

Starting with a loop on your hook, insert hook in stitch or space specified and draw up a loop (two loops on hook). Yarn over and pull yarn through both the loops on your hook (first sc made).

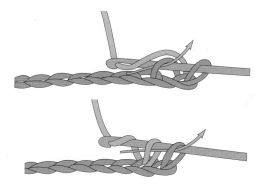

The height of a single crochet stitch is one chain high.

When working single crochet stitches into a foundation chain, begin the first single crochet in the second chain from the hook. The skipped chain stitch provides the height of the stitch.

At the beginning of a single crochet row or round, start by making one chain stitch (to get the height) and work the first single crochet stitch into first stitch (Note: The one chain stitch is never counted as a single crochet stitch).

HALF-DOUBLE CROCHET (hdc)

Starting with a loop on your hook, yarn over hook before inserting hook in stitch or space specified and draw up a loop (three loops on hook). Yarn over and pull yarn through all three loops (first hdc made).

The height of a half-double crochet stitch is two chains high.

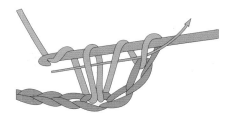

When working half-double crochet stitches into a foundation chain, begin the first stitch in the third chain from the hook. The two skipped chains provide the height. When starting a row or round with a half-double crochet stitch, make two chain stitches and work in the first stitch (Note: The two chain stitches are never counted as a half-double stitch).

DOUBLE CROCHET (dc)

Starting with a loop on your hook, yarn over hook before inserting hook in stitch or space specified and draw up a loop (three loops on hook). Yarn over and pull yarn through two loops (two loops remain on hook). Yarn over and pull yarn through remaining two loops on hook (first dc made).

The height of a double crochet stitch is three chains high.

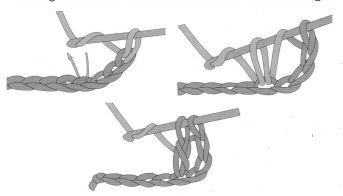

When working double crochet stitches into a foundation chain, begin the first stitch in the fourth chain from the hook.

The three skipped chains count as the first double crochet stitch. When starting a row or round with a double crochet stitch, make three chain stitches (which count as the first double crochet), skip the first stitch (under the chains) and work a double crochet in the next (second) stitch. On the following row or round, when you work in the 'made' stitch, you will be working in the top chain (3rd chain stitch of the three chains).

TREBLE (OR TRIPLE) CROCHET (tr)

Starting with a loop on your hook, yarn over hook twice before inserting hook in stitch or space specified and draw up a loop (four loops on hook). Yarn over and pull yarn through two loops (three loops remain on hook). Again, make a yarn over and pull yarn through two loops (two loops remain on hook). Once more, yarn over and pull through remaining two loops (first tr made).

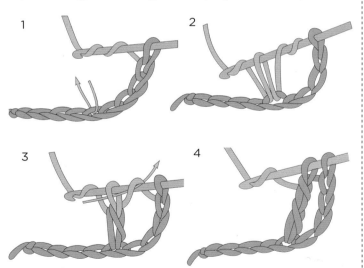

The height of a treble crochet stitch is four chains high.

When working treble crochet stitches into a foundation chain, begin the first stitch in the fifth chain from the hook. The four skipped chains count as the first treble crochet stitch. When starting a row or round with a

treble crochet stitch, make four chain stitches (which count as the first treble crochet), skip the first stitch (under the chains) and work a treble crochet in the next (second) stitch. On the following row or round, when you work in the 'made' stitch, you will be working in the top chain (4th chain stitch of the four chains).

DOUBLE TREBLE (OR DOUBLE TRIPLE) CROCHET (dtr)

Starting with a loop on your hook, yarn over hook three times before inserting hook in stitch or space specified and draw up a loop (five loops on hook). *Yarn over and pull yarn through two loops; rep from * three times more (until only the loop on your hook remains (first dtr made).

The height of a double treble crochet stitch is five chains high.

HEIGHT OF CHAIN STITCHES

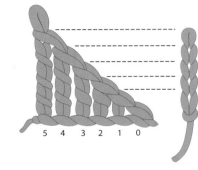

5 Double Treble Crochet
4 Treble Crochet
3 Double Crochet
2 Half-Double Crochet
1 Single Crochet
0 Slip Stitch

Crochet Techniques

MAGIC RING

Instead of starting with a ring consisting of a number of chain stitches, one can use a Magic Ring.

You start as if you were making a slip knot: Form a loop with your yarn (the tail end hanging behind your loop); insert the hook through the loop, and pick up the ball end of the yarn. Draw yarn through loop. Here is where things change... Do not tighten up the knot or loop. Make a chain stitch (to 'lock' the ring), then continue with the 'height' chain stitches. Work the required stitches into the ring (over the tail strand). When all the stitches are done, gently tug the tail end to close the ring, before joining the round (if specified). Remember, make sure this tail is firmly secured when weaving in the end.

STANDING STITCHES

Standing stitches replace the normal "join a new color (or yarn) with a slip stitch to the stitch or space specified and then chain up to the stitch height". They are made by working the stitch from the top-down.

Single Crochet Standing Stitch (join with sc)

With slip knot on hook, insert hook into stitch or space indicated and pull up a loop (two loops on hook). Yarn over and pull through both loops on hook (first single crochet made).

Half-Double Crochet Standing Stitch

With slip knot on hook, yarn over, (holding the two loops with thumb) insert hook into stitch or space indicated and pull up a loop (three loops on hook). Yarn over and pull through all three loops (standing half-double crochet made).

Double Crochet Standing Stitch

With slip knot on hook, yarn over, (holding the two loops with thumb) insert hook into stitch or space indicated and pull up a loop (three loops on hook). Yarn over and pull through two loop (two loops on hook). Yarn over and pull through remaining two loops (standing double crochet made).

CHANGING COLORS / ATTACHING NEW YARN

Changing to a new ball of yarn or a new color, ideally should happen when starting a new row or round.

Instead of fastening off one color and then joining a new color with a slip stitch or Standing Stitch, one can use the following technique:

In the stitch before the change, work up to last step of the stitch (In most cases the last step of a stitch is the final "yarn over, pull through remaining stitches on hook").

This is where the change happens. Here you will use the new color in the "yarn over" and pull it through the remaining stitches.

This technique is not only used for color changing. It can also be used to introduce a new ball of yarn (of the same color) while working on a project.

BACK RIDGE OF FOUNDATION CHAIN

Most projects start with a foundation chain – a string of chain stitches. One can identify the front of the chain stitches by seeing 'v's. When you turn the foundation chain over, at the back are a string of 'bumps'. This is referred to as the back ridge (or back bar) of the chain.

When working in the back ridge of the chain stitches, one inserts the hook from front to back through the 'bar' (the 'v' is underneath the hook) and pulls the yarn through the 'bar'.

Working your first row in the back ridge of the foundation chain, gives a neat finish to your project. If you are seaming pieces together, it also creates a flatter seam.

FRONT AND BACK LOOPS

Each stitch has what we call 'v's on the top. Unless otherwise specified, all stitches are worked by inserting the hook under both the loops – under the 'v'.

Sometimes a pattern calls for stitches worked in either the front or back loops. These are the two loops that make up the 'v'. The front loops are the loops closest to you and the back loops are the loops furthest from you. Working in the front or back loops only, creates a decorative ridge (of the unworked loops).

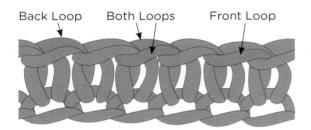

Back Loop   Both Loops   Front Loop

BLOCKING

To give your crochet creations a beautiful and professional look, it is advisable to block them all when finished. You can also block motifs before joining them together.

Wet-blocking is done by pinning out your piece to size and shape (using non-rust pins) on a clean, flat and soft surface. You can use towels, foam board, or rubber mat tiles.

Depending on the yarn you used, you can gently wash your crochet pieces first and then pin them out, or you can pin out the dry pieces, and lightly spritz them with water, or (if they are NOT acrylic) hover a steam iron over them. Never let the iron touch the crochet pieces. Leave the pinned pieces to dry completely.

CRAB STITCH

This stitch is also known as Reverse Single Crochet (rev-sc) and creates a neat edging to a project. It is similar to the regular single crochet stitch but is worked in the opposite direction – left to right (for right-handers) and right to left (for left-handers).

With a loop on the hook, * insert hook in next st to the right (or left for left-handers) and pull up loop, yarn over and pull through both loops on hook. Repeat from * across (or around).

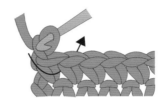
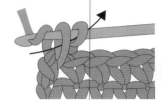

About the Author

Tanya Eberhardt is a frequent contributor to crochet books and magazines published in Europe and the US.

Her own blog **Little Things Blogged** is a place for all things crochet and yarn, updated regularly with free patterns and crochet information.

She also creates crochet and knitting patterns for her Little Things Blogged Etsy shop.